To Anar,

All the Best!

Ten Stocks
That Could Change
THE WORLD

Ten Stocks
That Could Change
THE WORLD

Larry Waschka
with
Greg Combs, CFA
Robert Bacon
Charles Martin, PhD, CFA

WCI Publishing
LITTLE ROCK

The authors wish to dedicate this book to our clients.

Published 2001 by WCI Publishing,
1501 N. University, Suite 557,
Little Rock, Arkansas, 72207,
www.waschka.com

Printed in the United States of America.

10 9 8 7 6 5 4 3 2 1 HB

Project Editor: Jody McNeese Keene
Cover Artist: Patrick McKelvey
Copyeditor: Bill Jones

Acknowledgements

I would like to personally thank my co-authors who focused so hard on this project, enabling us to finish in record time. Thank you for your enthusiasm, hard work, dedication, and friendship. Thanks also for making this so fun!

Larry

Together we would like to thank:

Page Atkins, for countless hours of fantastic editing and moral support for us all—without you, this would not have been possible.

We'd also like to thank our teammates at WCI for all of your support—all for one and one for all!

We'd like to give a special thanks to our literary agent, Ron Goldfarb, for all his help, advice, guidance, and empathy.

We'd like to thank Joseph Foote for his altruism and support.

And we'd like to thank Donna Harris for all her help, enthusiasm, foresight, ideas, and friendship. You have a promising career as an agent!

Contents

Introduction

A \$5,000 investment in the IPO (initial public offering) of Dell, Cisco, AOL, or Qualcomm would have made one a millionaire *five to ten times over* in less than a decade! Fortunately, *it is not too late* for you to see profits like this. These companies are not the only ones making a significant impact on the world economy. Many people feel it's too late—and they could not be further from the truth. There are many stocks out there trying their best to change some niche or segment of the world. Finding the right ones to buy is the problem, as there are thousands to choose from!

This book is about finding stocks that could change the world and have the potential of being world leaders five to ten years from now. We've identified the most significant revolutionary changes in the world today. These changes are revolutionary because they produce powerfully disruptive technologies. We're looking for revolutions big enough to produce new industries, which are capable of extraordinary growth rates. We then identify the stocks that have the best potential of bringing that technology to the marketplace and simultaneously produce significant profits for its shareholders.

The companies we've listed here are not the typical dot-coms that everyone rushed to buy in 1998 and 1999. These companies are unique because each one is a platform for a new industry. They are the infrastructure upon which these new industries can grow. In other words, these are the stocks that have a better chance of weathering the short-term volatility storms we've experienced recently. They are also unique in their leadership, vision, and scope of their individual markets.

Please Be Advised

Remember that the title is "Ten Stocks that COULD Change the World." We do not claim to have a crystal ball, we cannot tell the future, and we most certainly cannot and will not make any promises about the future of these stocks. We do promise, however, that we have thoroughly researched the fastest-growing industries to find a handful of stocks that have the potential of making a major global impact by providing a platform (infrastructure) of service or products upon which other companies can benefit.

Throughout the book, there are disclaimers regarding the risk these stocks carry with them. Some of these companies may not be able to keep up with the changes in their respective industries and may not exist by 2005. Therefore, it's important that investors be prudent about how much of their portfolios are committed to these stocks. These stocks are VERY AGGRESSIVE. Price swings of 60% in a few months are not uncommon. A look at their price movements from the first week of March 2000, until May 2000, will confirm this.

Stocks that are this aggressive together should represent no more than 10% of a moderate-risk portfolio. A very aggressive investor, with at least a ten-year time horizon, may want to increase this percentage.

Our efforts are meant to help investors narrow their searches from an overwhelming number to a handful of ideas for their portfolios. We encourage investors to do their own research and be smart when buying the stock.

Part I, "How to Find Stocks That Could Change the World," provides a condensed and easy to understand explanation of the changes (revolutions) the world is experiencing. With these concise yet thorough explanations, the reader will grasp the enormous potential of certain global industries. This section is designed to help our readers learn how to invest so they can prosper for a lifetime.

Part II, "Ten Stocks That Could Change the World," identifies the fastest-growing industries in the world and narrows the search down to ten stocks that have the potential to change the world.

Part III, "An Added Bonus," has two chapters. The first identifies ten larger stocks that are currently changing the world. The second reminds the reader that these stocks should represent only a portion of their over-all balanced portfolio. These companies are changing rapidly and investing heavily in the future. The industries are still evolving at a quick pace and the individual stocks are quite volatile. It is one thing to know which stocks can change the world. It's another to know when to buy them. Many of these stocks are over-priced at any given time. The final chapter of the book explains how to buy these stocks when they are "reasonably" priced.

Each of the stocks listed in this book has the potential to be a global brand name leader in a new technology that could live for decades, creating more wealth for investors than ever before.

How to Find Stocks
That Could
Change the World

The Real Secret of
Successful Investing?

Henry Ford invented the Model T in 1908. He produced one every 12½ hours. By 1925, he was producing one every ten seconds—and that is after improving the assembly line for nine years. Over the years, the price of a Model T dropped from $850 to $260, and Ford sold 15.4 million of them!

In the early 1900s, there were many automobile companies. The industry was in its innovation stage, just like the Internet is today. There were many startups and making a choice wasn't easy. There were hundreds of automobile manufacturers trying to get a product on the market, making for tight competition (and very difficult stock picking). Most of the manufacturing was concentrated in Detroit.

A $2,500 investment in Ford stock in 1903 would be worth a whopping $29 million in just 16 years!

There are two reasons why that information is key to this book. First, the Internet, bandwidth, wireless, and genomic revolutions offer the same opportunity *right now*. Second, during the early 1900s, electricity was the "general purpose technology which irreversibly transforms production" and built enormous fortunes for many inventors, businessmen, and investors. *(Electricity in the American Economy*, S. H. Schurr, C. C. Burwell, W.D. Devine, and S. Sonenblum, eds., Greenwood Press, 1990.)

Today's general-purpose technologies include the Internet, expanding bandwidth, and wireless technologies. Within the biotechnology field, the general-purpose technology would be genomics. Each one of these will be responsible for building great fortunes for many investors.

Many economists and market forecasters say the market and the economy can't continue to grow at recent high levels. They fear a recession or major market correction. The problem is that they are using 100-year data—stock market track record, economic growth rates and inflation—as a comparison to what's going on today. This is a major mistake. The only meaningful comparison would be to the early 1900s when electricity was the new general-purpose technology storming the country.

An even greater parallel understanding of today's stock market can be specifically found in the decade of the 1920s—not by rehashing "causes" for the 1929 crash, but by examining innovations that produced the growth economy of the 1920s.

Electric Power: The General Purpose Technology of the 1920s

Radio, movies, passenger airplanes, skyscrapers, mass-produced automobiles, cellophane, antifreeze, rayon, etc., were all important products of the 1920s economy, but none were vital. The growth in the use of electric power was the key. (*The Great Bull Market: Wall Street in the 1920s,* Robert Sobel, New York, 1968, p. 36)

- Completion of the first large hydroelectric dam at Niagara Falls in 1895 establishes alternating current as the U.S. standard for electric power distribution. (In current economic parlance, electricity becomes a "general purpose technology" which irreversibly transforms production. See *Electricity in the American Economy,* S.H. Schurr, C.C. Burnwell, W.D. Devine, and S. Sonenblum, eds. (Greenwood Press, 1990).
- In 1919, 32 percent of factory machinery was powered by electricity; by 1929 the figure was 49 percent.
- During the 1920s the number of kilowatt-hours *per capita* in the U.S. rose 89%.
- By 1929 the United States was producing more electric power than the rest of the world combined. The *per capita* production (productivity) of the American worker was 60% higher than it had been thirty years earlier.

"The application of this [electric] power in old industries, internal reorganizations within the industries, rapid expansion of foreign markets, and, most important, the introduction of new techniques of marketing and mass distribution, helped make the twenties an era of growth and gave the decade its glow of prosperity." (Robert Sobel, *The Great Bull Market: Wall Street in the 1920s*, New York, 1968, p. 36.)

During the early 1900s, inventors were hard at work devising and producing home appliances and all the basic electric gadgets we take for granted today. Suddenly, the number of patents issued skyrocketed, as well as the number of companies going public. The economy boomed and brought the Roaring Twenties. Electricity swept the country, electrifying homes and businesses. This long-term fundamental trend spawned many other inevitable trends. What's important to learn from these historical events is that long-term fundamental trends are rarely so plentiful during any one single decade. General-purpose technology trends like electricity can produce huge investment opportunities, some of which may last many generations.

The stock market values created in the 1920s were unprecedented. The real question is whether the 1920s "vintage" capital survived. Was the vast stock market value created in the bull market lost with the crash or is that value still vital to today's economy? These are questions long-term investors should be asking when they observe the run up of today's new economy stocks and question the permanence of these new technologies and their high market capitalizations.

It is easy to make ad hoc comparisons. One needs look only at the story of RCA (Radio Corporation of America) to initially feel a bit uneasy about a present-day Microsoft or AOL.

In 1919, at the urging of the U.S. Navy, General Electric (GE) formed a privately owned corporation to acquire the assets of the wireless Radio Company, American Marconi, from British Marconi. British Marconi was poised to purchase patented alternator technology from GE and the Navy was concerned that future development of a key information medium might then become monopolized by a foreign power. The Navy pressured General Electric to pool its patents with Westinghouse and AT&T to form a radio cartel. The resulting company was incorporated as Radio Corporation of America (RCA) and soon became the darling of Wall Street.

- 1921—RCA trades as low as $1.50/share in the OTC market
- 1922—High-$6.25/share
- 1924—High-$66 7/8 after a 1 for 5 reverse stock split
- 1925—High-$77 7/8. The compound rate of return on RCA from 1921-1925 was 72%/year and the company paid no dividends! Taxes, compared to today, were insignificant.
- 1925-1929—RCA continues to grow at a phenomenal rate— 47.2%/year between 1925 and 1929
- 1929—RCA goes above $400/share and peaks before the crash at $114 3/4 after a 5 for 1 stock split

In the early 1930s, the Justice Department filed an antitrust suit against RCA. In a 1932 consent decree, GE, AT&T, and Westinghouse agreed to sell their interests in RCA, thus forcing it to become an independent company. Even though RCA still held all its key patents and owned NBC, the shares of RCA hit an all-time low of $3/share in 1932, a 97% drop from the 1929 high. Does this sound familiar?

One can look today (December 2000) at Microsoft or AOL with their price drops and Microsoft's antitrust suit and draw some potentially nerve-wracking historical analogies. The point is that in spite of the crash and antitrust suits, RCA/GE is still around today.

Under the leadership of David Sarnoff, RCA spent millions in the 1930s on television research and patent buyouts. They arrived at the 1939 World's Fair in New York with the first line of consumer televisions. The rest *is* history and little more need be reported here about RCA, except to note that GE again acquired it in 1986. But the story for investors in GE itself—another Wall Street darling of the 1920s—is worth a brief look:

- 1929—GE peaks at $403/sh. EPS is reported at $8.97 for 1929. P/E= 44.93.
- 2000—EPS is reported at $1.22. P/E 49.8.

Were the investors who thought GE was worth forty-five times earnings in 1929 insane? They were insane only if they knew about the upcoming depression. However, they weren't wrong considering the long-run fundamental value of the company.

The real secret of successful investing is systematically investing in long-term, fundamental trends—three-, five-, and ten-year series of events that have clear levels of global significance socially, politically, and economically.

Blindly predicting the future is a pointless exercise, especially when it comes to money. However, there is great value to studying the past as a tool in identifying likely scenarios for the future. By imagining the possibilities and careful, continuous research, an investor has a good shot at making a sound prediction of what might come. It may be frustrating, but it can still be a valuable thing to attempt. First imagine the possibilities. Then select the most probable scenarios. Most of the allure of these companies is the vision of the leadership. Almost all of the CEOs of the companies listed here have a vision to change the world.

To know something about the future, the past must be understood. Take a look at this list below. What do these items have in common?

The Wheel	Crop Rotation
Gun Powder	The Radio
The Printing Press	Steam Engine
Electricity	The Telephone
The Automobile	The Airplane
The Assembly-line	The Computer

What do these companies have in common?

AT&T	GE
Ford	Motorola
Boeing	IBM
McDonalds	Wal-Mart
Microsoft	AOL

The first is a list of things (past trends) that changed the world. The second is a list of companies that changed the world and made many people very rich. It's my belief that the Internet, along with the growing expansion of bandwidth, is more powerful than any of the above and will make even more people very, very rich.

In the 1990s, 259 stocks rose over 1,000%, while the top 20 *grew* more than 27,000%! By March of 2000, Dell rose 91,000%, Cisco rose

100,000%, AOL rose 66,000%, and Qualcomm 21,000%. A $5,000 investment would have made one a millionaire *five to ten times over* in less than a decade! It is our belief that the same thing will happen again in the first decade of the new millennium. There are opportunities in the market today that have similar capital gains potential.

Not so long ago, the greatest wealth-making engine in history, the Internet, was considered just a nerdy toy. Internet traffic is growing exponentially. George Gilder, author of *The Telecosm*, says, "Rising at least a thousand times every five years, the trajectory of [Internet] traffic indicates that a current Internet company is confronting just one tenth of one percent of its potential volume half a decade hence." The irony is that most investors feel that we've already experienced the bulk of what the Internet can bring—both in terms of usage and investment opportunity. John Patrick, VP of Internet Technology at IBM, says "We're right at the very beginning of what the Internet will make possible for the average person or business. *We're only about 2% or 3% in, and we haven't seen anything compared to what's coming!*" If George and John are right, we have in front of us one of, if not the best, investment opportunities in the history of the world. The irony is that most investors feel that we've already experienced the bulk of what the Internet can bring, both in terms of usage and investment opportunity.

Crises and Revolutions Creating a New Economy

According to most English thesauruses, the word "crisis" has the following synonyms: catastrophe, emergency, calamity, predicament and disaster. The Chinese language has a different definition. Their symbol for the word "crisis" is made up of two symbols, Wey and Che.

Wey means danger and Che means opportunity. The best investors understand that wherever there's danger, there is often opportunity. This book isn't just a list of ten stocks, it's a summary of world-changing, inevitable trends that are creating danger and opportunity all over the world. The stocks themselves are riding the trends.

The crisis we face today is an economic revolution that is forcing dramatic changes in the world. This economic revolution is being fueled by six concurrent revolutions:

- Computer revolution
- Information revolution
- Internet revolution
- Bandwidth revolution
- Wireless revolution
- Genomic revolution

Never in recorded history have there been so many world-changing innovations at one time. The way we do business, communicate, think, receive information, research, and live are all affected by these "revolutions." Old traditional barriers in communication, including the availability of information, are being broken down in all countries and within every social stratum. The world truly has become a "global village." The changes we've seen so far have been huge, but we haven't seen anything yet! There will be more of them in our lives during this decade than there have been over the last century.

Innovation is occurring at such a rapid rate, some are finding it difficult to adjust. Many people are still not ready to incorporate the new technologies in their daily lives. For example, according to a recent survey, over 62% of people were apprehensive about making credit card transactions over the Internet. Over 50% of the U.S. population is on-line, but only 20% of on-line users have bought anything on-line! There is all this wonderful technology available today, but people aren't accustomed to the innovations or the possibilities just yet. For many, it's a little like the cliché, "You can't teach an old dog new tricks." However, in time, the power of technology will overtake this fear of change.

Take a moment and look at how breakthroughs in technology are altering the way the world lives, works, and communicates. These changes are revolutionary changes, not evolutionary. As such, they are abrupt and they are inevitable. We've identified some of the new industries that are bringing us these changes, as well as the leading companies in these industries. This will help you build a "New Economy" portfolio that is diversified among these different industries.

I firmly believe, as do many influential CEOs, that this is just the dawn of the New Economy. The investment opportunities available today are rare. Economists want to compare today's economic environment to 100-year stock average market returns, average gross domestic-product growth rates, and inflation rates. It seems logical, but this decade is different. The only real comparison we have is the Roaring Twenties, when electricity was the newest general-purpose technology. Henry Ford invented the assembly line in 1914 and the U.S. economy was growing rapidly at that time. Patents were issued left and right. Companies were going public at a rate never seen before (and not seen again for decades.)

Many of these companies grew fast and made a lot of people a great deal of money. A number of these companies are still around today and have made multimillionaires out of the generations who've held on to these stocks! No other decade before 1960 produced this much in corporate equity. The same phenomenon is taking place again. We are seeing the Internet as the new general-purpose technology, which has spawned a record number of patents per million people and record number of companies going public. As with the stocks of the 1920s, many of these companies will be here for generations, but many of them will fail.

Just like in the Roaring Twenties, today's world is one of rapid change. The way the world communicates, does business, learns and lives has been affected by the innovations of the "digital age." The old barriers in communications are beginning to disappear. Today on the Internet, information on almost any subject is available twenty-four hours a day. It is as if everyone had an entire branch of the public library right at home, yet even better! Regardless of location, a connection to the Internet with 56.6k or better bandwidth, the world is brought to the computer screen. Suddenly, we really are a global village.

So how did we get here? Much of the credit should go to the companies who had the foresight and vision to produce the innovations that enabled us to connect to the Internet. These companies have changed the world and as a result, made many people VERY rich.

Current Revolutions Changing the World

Computer revolution

The computer revolution is not new. Moore's Law, named after Intel's founder Gordon Moore, states that microprocessor speeds double every eighteen months. From the first Intel chip to the most current one under development the Pentium IV (P-4), we've seen enormous progress in the speed at which computers operate. The historic progression looks like this:

Processor	Date Introduced	Clock Speed
8088	1979	5 Mhz
286	1982	8 MHz
386	1985	16 MHz
486	1989	25 MHz
Pentium	1993	60 MHz
Pentium Pro	1995	150 MHz
Pentium II	1997	233 MHz
Pentium III	1999	600 MHz
Pentium IV	2001	2 GHz (2,000 Mhz)

This revolution alone has advanced every human being's productivity level and, as a result, has helped corporations become much more profitable. Many experts believe that this revolution is expected to diminish in ten years when the microchip can't double in speed every eighteen months anymore. That fact certainly won't cripple the computer industry, considering the potential of the other revolutions listed here.

Information revolution

I remember my excitement with the coming information revolution that John Naisbet discussed in his book *Megatrends*. That concept states that the amount of power a person had in the world directly correlated to the amount of information he held and managed. Information became even more powerful when Microsoft went public and brought us software such as Works, Word, and Excel. Information is still power, and now the ability to connect to it is even greater.

The information revolution spawned many different mini-revolutions. Printing is a good example of an industry that made unbelievable strides due to the information revolution, and through its advances, other industries benefited. The following is a timeline of the development of printing:

Print revolution
Written page
Set type—newsprint
Typewritten page
Word Processing (Information revolution)
Networking (Information revolution)

The ability to do word processing and networking has transformed the way most businesses conduct their everyday activities.

Internet revolution

A tenth-grade high school student in Tyler, Texas, finds an on-line calculus tutor who uses proven techniques to raise knowledge and test scores to the highest percentile. An antique dealer, limited by the geographic confines of a small town in Tennessee, builds her own web site with pictures of her collection, and overnight she's selling to buyers in Tucson, Arizona. A man in Turkey builds his own personal home page using broken English, which is discovered by an artist in Memphis who thinks it's the funniest thing she's seen in her whole life. She quickly copies everyone in her e-mail list, who in turn copy all their friends. In two days the site has over one million hits. Three days later, the Turkish man is on ABC's *Good Morning America.*

The Internet has been around for a long time, but the invention of the browser has made it useful in a broad sense. The browser makes surfing the web possible. At first, the Internet was the greatest thing ever invented (and it probably is), but people soon became frustrated. The Internet is known as the World Wide Web (WWW). However, to many, it has become the World Wide Wait! Today, most people have 56kbs/second modems and have never experienced faster speeds. If you are fortunate enough to be one of the early ones to get a high-speed Internet connection (500kbs/sec or better), be warned that you will be the target of envy! All your family, friends and associates will want, demand and expect the same speed.

Let's consider the print industry once again.

Print revolution
Written page
Set type—newsprint
Typewritten page
Word Processing (Information revolution)
Networking (Information revolution)
Web page (Internet revolution)

The creation of the web page made it possible for anyone and everyone to express their thoughts in a global arena. This is just the beginning of the forthcoming advantages of the Internet Revolution. But the Internet Revolution is nothing without bandwidth.

Bandwidth revolution

And what is bandwidth? It's the Internet connection speed at which data can flow to and from your computer, cell phone, or other device.

As bandwidth is the amount of data measured in bits that can be transmitted in a fixed amount of time, the tools to make a fast, reliable connection possible are extremely important. The following examples demonstrate what is achievable after the "bandwidth revolution" is a world-wide reality.

A medical student in London sits in on a rare surgical procedure conducted in San Francisco performed by the best surgeon in the world. A businessman in his living room in Athens, Greece, buys a condo in Aspen after taking a full live tour of the facility given by his real estate agent—whom he's never met. A traveling businesswoman in New York has dinner together with her daughter in Chicago and her son in Bald Knob, Arkansas. A golfer in Shreveport, Louisiana, caught in the sand trap gets a lesson from Tiger Woods's web site using his smart phone, while his foursome pitches onto the green. Two men stuck in a boring meeting secretly play chess on their phones while pretending to take notes on the meeting.

A young couple on their honeymoon arrive in San Diego and their cell phone notifies them of three restaurants offering honeymooners 20% off their bill and confirms that each of the restaurants serve the couple's favorite foods and wines. So they then punch two for reservations, seven for a seven o'clock reservation, and five for a map, which they can refer to at anytime. Their phone also tells them that their favorite musician, Sting, is performing the next night and tickets are still available on the front row. The couple presses two to purchase and five for a map to the concert. Their itinerary is set within minutes of arriving in town and every transaction is automated and charged to their cell phone bill. This may all sound like fantasy, but it's very real—and this is only the beginning of what's to come.

These stories are only the start of what is possible with the coming bandwidth revolution. The bandwidth revolution is essential in making emerging technologies available and user-friendly to the average person.

Most on-line users today are connected by phone line to the Internet at 56.6 kbs/second or 56,600 bits per second. This is twice as fast as a 28kbs. This is a nice speed, but relative to what is potentially available, this is nothing. Industry experts say the maximum bandwidth capacity now for copper wire (phone line) is approximately 3 megabits or 3 million bits per second. The maximum bandwidth capacity for one single fiber-optic cable, with a width of one human hair, is 565 megabits or 565 million bits per second (and even higher by the time one reads this). Not even 1% of the U.S. population is using fiber-optic cable connected directly to a home or business. Currently, we are only using 2% of the capacity of what is technologically possible.

Suppose there is a house on fire, but only a simple garden hose to put it out. Considering the small amount of water that generally comes out of a hose, the house will likely burn down. But what if there were a fire hose connected to a pressurized pump truck? Not only would there be more water capacity because of the size of the hose, there would be even more water because of the pump. Bandwidth is similar to the water flow. Most people have the equivalent of a garden-hose connection to their computer. This will not be the case for long.

An Internet connection at one megabit/second would allow incredible streaming video, personal and professional videoconferencing, movies and encyclopedias on demand, and on and on. The only limit is imagination. The power of this connection is also directly proportionate to the number of other people connected at this same high speed (or better). With this technology, one could teach a class on a favorite subject, film it by digital video camera, and put it on a personal web site for others to see.

We have the bandwidth technology to make all this happen—it is just not evenly distributed yet. Given this discrepancy in capacity versus availability, it is easy to see the crises, as well as the opportunity. Those who address this opportunity could "change the world."

The primary tool the bandwidth industry will rely upon is fiber-optic cable, which is the fastest, clearest, least expensive, and lightest way to transmit huge amounts of data. Fiber-optic cables are also thinner and less susceptible than metal cables (phone and co-axial) to interference. They can also carry data in digital form—the same form used in the computer—rather than analog. The disadvantage of fiber-optic cable is that it's more fragile than wire. The glass fiber inside can be cracked if it is bent too far. Because it's glass, it's much more difficult to connect or split to a connection.

Fiber-optic cable is capable of 565 million bits per second. It's lighter, less expensive, and takes less space. The most important fact is that fiber-optic cable not only carries more data faster, it carries it at a fraction of the cost relative to copper wire. With today's technology, one single fiber-optic cable (the thickness of a human hair) has the ability to carry in one second all the Internet traffic that took place in an average month in 1997.

If the computer revolution was big with the microprocessor speeds doubling every eighteen months, imagine bandwidth speeds doubling every six months!

For many, the ultimate goal is a global fiber-optic network with every PC and phone capable of real-time live video stream and every call a video-conference. The result will be every PC and every phone connected to the web and capable of things only dreamt of today.

Bandwidth is the new general purpose technology, one which will lead to new technologies. There are a record number of new patents and record number of new business start-ups as a direct result. This will continue for several years as higher bandwidth goes mainstream into most homes and businesses. A successful technology investor must keep track of new advancements in the field.

The bandwidth revolution will be the catalyst for many industries to take that next revolutionary step that changes everything. For example, the bandwidth revolution takes the printing industry to a whole new world where the entire Library of Congress can be sent over the Internet in a matter of a second, and this includes high-resolution (data-hogging) graphics.

> Print revolution
> Written page
> Set type—newsprint
> Typewritten page
> Word Processing (Information revolution)
> Networking (Information revolution)
> Web page (Internet revolution)
> The entire Library of Congress sent in a second with high-resolution
>   graphics (Bandwidth revolution)

The bandwidth revolution will spawn more social and economic change than the computer revolution. Hence, the world will experience more change in the first ten years of the new millennium than we saw in the twentieth century. The opportunity for today's investor is identifying the handful of companies who will be the "bandwidth revolutionaries." Picking these companies is quite a complex, time-consuming challenge as there are many who will vie to be the leaders in the industry.

Wireless Revolution

With the expansion of bandwidth and wireless technology, cell phones will be used more for Internet access than PCs. These "third generation" phones will combine the technology of personal digital assistants (PDAs), Internet access, video teleconferencing, voice activation, paging, 2 way e-mail, Bluetooth (low frequency radio transmission), and the cell phone. They will be a remote control for one's life and will change the old perceptions of telecommunications. Such technology is already available in Scandinavia and Japan. What's happening there is nothing short of a lifestyle revolution. Children buy a coke from a machine with their phone, they play games against each other on their phones, trade Mp3 files, and communicate with e-mail. We will see this in the U.S. by the end of 2001.

Take a look again at the print industry and the change brought about by all these revolutions.

> Print revolution
> Written page
> Set type—newsprint
> Typewritten page
> Word Processing (Information revolution)
> Networking (Information revolution)
> Web page (Internet revolution)
> The entire Library of Congress sent in a second with high-resolution
>   graphics (Bandwidth revolution)
> Web page on a cell phone (Wireless revolution)

The question now is "What's next?" If you think that this is the last change, think again. How about a voice-activated interactive web page on your phone? That's an easy prediction. The harder ones take knowledge and imagination.

Genomic revolution

A glimpse into the future of medicine might look like this:

An MIT biotech resident learns the latest developments in prostate cancer therapy from a biotech company's on-line "Genomic University" offered free on their web site twenty-four hours a day. From his home in Seattle, a physician uses a genomic company's web site to download a portion of the human genome and discovers a possible cure for melanoma. A woman in Montreal with breast cancer takes an experimental gene therapy drug in phase-three trials and is completely cured of cancer without any radiation or surgery. Using a tiny silicon bio-chip, a professor at the University of Arkansas Medical Center works together with a physician in Geneva to discover the proteomix that spawns a whole new generation of gene therapy for muscular dystrophy. News agencies around the world fight to be the first to announce all of the new drugs that consistently come to market. Imagine life expectancies of 120 and beyond!

This may all seem unbelievable, but not to the many genomic companies that have just started up or to their shareholders.

On Monday, June 26, 2000, the world of medicine experienced a huge leap into the future. Two parties, one corporate and one government, announced the mapping of the human genome. We now have a blueprint of the human genetic make-up and the role genes play in health and behavior. It means that the race has begun to develop gene therapy drugs that can cure genetic mistakes such as cystic fibrosis and colon cancer. In addition, the pace of drug development will increase at least five times faster. Genomic companies have two basic functions. First, they serve as a library or database of the human genome map from which other biotech companies purchase data for further research. Second, they develop gene-therapy drugs. FDA approval (which is never guaranteed) for the first gene-therapy drugs is more than likely a few years away.

Currently, there are over three hundred biotech companies that are publicly traded and twenty have positive cash flow. There are about one thousand not yet public and over forty IPOs expected in the first few months of 2001. This is a very hot sector and will likely become overvalued, just like Internet companies. They will be extremely volatile, but the trend will continue and the best companies will rise to the top. Unfortunately, the FDA's phase-three trial of a drug often costs hundreds of millions of dollars. If the FDA doesn't approve a certain drug, then that developing company could go bankrupt. As an investor, it's important to understand the risk here—it is real and it is significant. However, if an investor does her homework and finds companies that are diversifying their income stream—not just focusing on one drug—she may make a lot of money.

There are two types of biotech companies: traditional biotech and genomic companies. The first group is full of companies with positive cash flow. The second group can only dream of cash flow in the future. Over time, the second group will produce a handful of winners that could make many people very rich.

Today's elderly are becoming pioneers in time, because they're living longer with a better quality of life than any other generation. Genomics will certainly contribute to this phenomenon by profoundly accelerating drug development and improving the quality of life for millions of people.

The New Economy

Take all these revolutions and their combined effect on the economy, and you have the ingredients for a new economy where nothing is stationary. The way we research, shop, buy, think, interact with others, illustrate, find information, learn, work, and market goods will change. It seems like a century of change happened in only a decade. This is why comparisons between the Old Economy and New Economy are heard so often.

The New Economy is currently attacking the Old Economy and old ways of thinking. For example, consider the financial markets in which large institutions and investors have all the inside information and therefore get a jump on the best of investments and prices on goods. This "good ole boy network" is slowly fading and giving way to a fairer market where anyone has equal ability to bid on what they want in the market. Wit/Soundview is a great example of a New Economy company. They take companies public and their IPO market is open to anyone who wants to make a bid. This has been a highly welcomed shift in the way IPOs are sold. In the New Economy, people demand a fair marketplace, no matter what they are buying.

eBay has been so successful because Pierre Omidyar created the first big auction site on the web and transformed the Internet into a giant garage sale that happens to make money.

The Internet is relatively uncharted territory, and the transportation system (bandwidth) is in the early stages of development. The Internet along with good bandwidth is bigger than a land grab. Imagine a land grab with an infinite amount of land available and towns popping up all over the world.

It can be safely said that the growth in output and profitability of the New Economy is staggering. According to some widely publicized estimates, output per worker growth in the New Economy manufacturers is 30%, which is twelve times higher than Old Economy output. New Economy profit growth is 58%, which is over seven times higher than Old Economy profit growth.

It is estimated that the New Economy as a percentage of the U.S. economy was approximately 20% in 1999 and earned almost half of all the national corporate profits. It is even more amazing that many of the forecasting entities are predicting that the New Economy will make up 50% of the U.S. economy by 2008, and 75% of the economy by 2010! If this is true and if our portfolios should reflect what the market looks like in the future, most investors have a lot of rearranging to do.

Identifying
the Best Sectors
and the Best Stocks

At my farm, I have a huge walnut tree that has been around for several generations. It stands out in the open and every year it sees its fair share of high winds, rain, snow, and hundred-degree heat. After every storm, I'll find small branches that break off in the wind. The larger branches they connect to rarely ever break off. One day, I was driving home thinking about the stocks I wanted to buy in my portfolio. When I pulled into my farmhouse, there on the ground were several small branches that had fallen off in a storm that afternoon.

The market is much like a tree. The trunk of the tree represents the larger blue-chip companies in the market. From there, the largest limbs branch out into the medium-size limbs, which branch out to feed the smaller and smallest limbs. These medium-size limbs are like medium-size stocks. They've been around for a while and don't tend to fall off the tree as easy as the smaller ones. They also tend to feed the smaller limbs. Why not buy the medium-size companies that are feeding the smaller ones?

I call these stocks "platform" or "infrastructure" stocks. They are the stage upon which the other smaller companies perform their magic. They are the infrastructure upon which other companies are built. These stocks provide other companies the products, services, or information they need to service their customers.

For example, the biggest problem with the Internet today is speed. People have become frustrated with the World Wide Wait. More bandwidth is the solution, especially as more and more people around the world get "connected." Initially that means cable modems and DSL lines, which are often 200 times faster than a lot of connections today. Who would voluntarily choose a slower connection? Eventually, we'll have fiber-optic cable into our homes and offices, which is "the last mile" of the Internet. This will mean, again, speeds 200 times faster than DSL…and that is fast! THE question for the smart investor is: "What stock will give us this bandwidth?" The answer is a bandwidth infrastructure company.

Other questions for the investor:

- What are today's most significant discoveries?
- Which of them have the greatest potential to change the world?
- What new industries are emerging today to produce these discoveries?
- What industries do you see experiencing radical, revolutionary change?
- Which of these industries will grow the fastest?
- Are there sub-groups within these industries?
- Can their market potential be found using the Internet?
- Which companies are the leaders in each industry?
- Which ones have patents and licenses?
- Which one got there first?

Listed below are a few of our favorite industries. Each one is experiencing radical, revolutionary change and super-high revenue growth. These certainly are not the only industries growing rapidly, but they are ones to watch.

- Digital rights management and watermarking
- B2B or business to business
- Web-conference/meeting
- Internet content delivery
- Undersea Fiber-Optic Network
- eLearning
- Photonics
- Genomics

Each of these industries was nonexistent as little as five years ago. Currently, the smallest industry is digital rights management, which may become a one-billion-dollar business in five years. The largest is B2B, which is expected to grow into a two to six trillion-dollar business by 2003.

Each of these industries is made up of many sub-groups that have relatively different rates of growth potential. For example, Business-to-Business E-Commerce could include e-purchasing software, e-conference software/web space, and e-commerce service software.

The next step is to identify the sub-groups in each of these industries and identify the leaders in each sub-group.

The Selection Criteria

It has been said that a monkey throwing darts can build a great portfolio. To prove that we don't have a monkey on staff, we thought we should show the parameters that we used to select the companies.

Once all of the industries are organized and identified by their potential markets, then we select the best stocks. We don't just accept the leader, we take them through a checklist of our criteria once again to insure we have a potential winner.

It's important to remember that we did not pay any attention to pricing. Some of these companies are outrageously priced. Be sure to read the last chapter regarding the buying process. It's one thing to know about a stock that could change the world. It's another thing to know when to buy it and when to sell.

Ability to change the world

Does the stock have the potential to change the world? Does the CEO want to change the world? Ideally, we want to find a stock that has a significant global impact. It may be that the company changes the way we do business, communicate, think, receive information, research, and live. It may be that the company is helping to facilitate a trend that in and of itself is changing the world in a measurable way.

Sector potential—Potential market size

We look for stocks that have (or could have) a product or service that will be in demand within five years as a part of a particular unfolding trend. We focus our search on the emerging trends that have the biggest potential markets. For example, eLearning is an industry that will truly change the world. However, very few people understand the possibilities and trends that are taking place today, much less what is possible tomorrow, as more people get connected at higher bandwidth rates. Today, in this industry, there are very few "players" that are publicly traded. If we believe that this could be a $100 billion business within three years, we know that it doesn't take a rocket scientist to buy both stocks and ride the wave.

Platform or Infrastructure for other companies

Does this stock provide a platform or infrastructure through which other companies can benefit? We don't necessarily want the company selling something to the consumer—we want the company to help many other companies sell to the consumer. We want the industry leader who is providing the key platform of the process and we want them to focus completely on delivering the best platform in the world.

Potential to be a world leader in five years

Could this stock be the global brand-name leader in five to ten years in its fast-growing industry? Ideally, we want to own the top brands or leaders in an industry that is growing unusually fast.

Revenue growth

Does the stock have revenue growth that exceeds 50% per year? We look for dramatically expanding revenues and will favor companies and industries with the highest growth rates in revenues. Can this pace continue in the near future? Many of these stocks do not have earnings yet. Therefore, it's important to have super-high revenue growth to at least provide the hope that earnings will follow.

Earnings growth/progression (losing less money each year relative to gross income)

Most of these companies have no earnings because they are growing so fast. What we want to see is at least some indication that this will end in the future. Therefore, what would be ideal is a situation where the company is losing less money each year as a percentage of gross income. This would mean that the company has a better chance of being profitable in the near future. In other words, we would at least like to see light at the end of the tunnel.

Recurring revenues

Once the company gets customers, do they receive regular income from them? Is their revenue from each customer recurring? We want to buy companies who get paid by their clients every year for their service. With every new client, more recurring revenue is added to the income statement.

Management depth—experience, accomplishments

The key to all highly successful companies is their leadership. Does management have what it takes to execute their vision? Where did these people come from and what have they accomplished in their past? This is the only track record for many of these new companies.

A few more things we considered include: barriers to entry or competition, strategic alliances/partners, gross margins, and debt.

Ten Stocks
That Could
Change the World

Digital Rights Management

Digimarc Corporation
Securing the Future of Commerce

Digital-Rights Management and Watermarking

With the widespread availability of cheap and ever more powerful computer technology, it is easier than ever before to make counterfeit copies of currency, financial instruments, copyrighted photographs, or more mundane items such as tickets for sporting events. High-resolution scanners and printers combined with inexpensive digital-imaging technology enable even relatively inexperienced users to produce professional-looking copies of identity documents or photographs. According to International Data Corporation (IDC) estimates, "worldwide scanner shipments will increase at 23.3% per year to 39.5 million units by 2003 and worldwide PC camera shipments will grow from approximately 600,000 in 1997 to more than 9.2 million units by 2002." (Digimarc Prospectus, 1999, p. 31) This dramatic expansion of imaging technology creates a demand for the company's copyright-protection technology and will also help build a market for its MediaBridge application. MediaBridge will interface with most scanners and with PC cameras from major manufacturers such as Intel, Phillips, and 3Com.

The rise of e-commerce and the increasing ease with which digital information can be transmitted around the globe will also increase demand for copy protection of digital media. We believe that Digimarc will emerge as a key enabler in further expanding e-commerce by allowing content providers to distribute their product in digital format without the constraint of worrying over potential losses from pirating. In fact, we believe that Digimarc's applications offer the most robust protection available because their watermark codes are invisible to the naked eye, persistent and format-independent (i.e., they can operate in either digital or analog media). Even resizing (within limits) of the image or transfer from digital to analog (or the reverse) will not disable the watermark protection.

Introduction

Digimarc is at the forefront of two important trends that will reshape the way we do business and protect against piracy and counterfeiting. The company is already a leader in the use of digital watermarking technologies to deter currency counterfeiting and pirating of photographic images. Digimarc is now also marketing a new service called MediaBridge that will enable consumers to instantly access a specific web site by simply scanning in a watermark from a magazine ad, business card, etc. These applications are merely a starting point but they serve as meaningful examples of the long-term potential that Digimarc's patented technologies can eventually realize.

Company History and Description

Digimarc is a trailblazer in digital-rights management. The company began filing for patents in 1993 and has since established a very broad portfolio of 22 issued and 160 pending U.S. patents. Digimarc has also filed for a number of foreign patent applications, and they are defending their rights vigorously, as evidenced by three lawsuits they filed in early 2000. In 1996, Digimarc began offering its digital watermark to photographers and leading stock photo agencies. The company's stock photo customers account for approximately 75% of all stock photo collections including more than 60 million high-quality photographs. These relationships also helped Digimarc develop other products such as the MarcSpider service, which allows owners of copyrighted material to track its distribution over the Internet and catch pirated copies.

The next major development for Digimarc was winning a multi-year contract from a consortium of leading central banks to apply its digital watermark technology to deter the use of personal computers in currency counterfeiting. Digimarc should also realize increasing revenue from this system when issuing authorities other than central banks begin licensing it to protect non-bank note value documents like passports and travelers' checks. This contract currently supplies the majority of Digimarc's revenues.

Digimarc's next major goal is to establish its digital watermarking technology as a key component in the future of e-commerce. There is a major push underway to gain adoption of the company's MediaBridge connected-content system, which, among other things, allows consumers to use printed media as a direct and seamless bridge to access the Internet. Digimarc's MediaBridge technology is well-positioned to fight for the lead in this rapidly developing market. Digimarc enjoys the backing of several large technology firms including Adobe, Hewlett Packard, Macrovision, and Philips N.V., and has also received financing from Reuters, Ltd. The company's watermark reader software will be included with most leading brands of web cameras, including Intel PC Cameras, and works with most of the already-installed base of scanners. Additionally, the company is participating in the Millennium group (Macrovision, Royal Phillips Electronics and Digimarc) that has proposed a comprehensive anti-piracy initiative for digital-to-digital video copy protection to the motion-picture industry.

MediaBridge

The next step in the company's development has already begun. It has signed up publishers that represent over 160 magazines (see table below for some of the leading magazines involved) with over 150 million readers to use its new MediaBridge technology as a link from print media directly to the web. Advertisers are waking up to the obvious potential inherent in using the Internet to reach customers. According to IDC estimates, the number of Internet users will expand to 320 million on a global basis by 2002 from 104 million in 1998. The expected increase in consumers who will actually make purchases on the web is even greater with IDC predicting 128 million in 2002 up from 18 million in 1997. This is all very exciting, but the idea that makes MediaBridge so attractive is the convenience that it offers as the Internet becomes more crowded and difficult to navigate (particularly for novice users).

Leading Magazines Licensed for Digimarc-Enabled Ads

Good Housekeeping	*People*	*Smart Money*
Sports Illustrated	*Seventeen*	*Popular Mechanics*
Wired	*Scientific American*	*Time*

The amount of information on the web is growing explosively: "NEC estimates that the number of web pages will increase from 320 million in 1997 to 9.1 billion in 2002." (Prospectus, p. 32) However, actually finding the relevant data that a user seeks is growing more complicated. As estimated by NEC, "the most comprehensive search engine indexes less than 16% of the web, a decrease from previous periods. NEC also estimates that the top 11 search engines combined currently index only 42% of the web." (Prospectus, p. 33) With MediaBridge the consumer can instantly and easily transfer from a printed ad to a related web site. Also, advertisers can offer special promotions that are targeted to readers of a particular magazine, such as a discount on Bosch parts for readers of *Popular Mechanics*. A company could design a web site so that only people with the printed ad would be able to access it. The fact is that magazines are already a significant source of web traffic. "A MarketFacts survey indicates that in 1998 approximately 62% of current Internet users visited a web site after seeing it mentioned in a magazine or newspaper." (Prospectus, p. 33) We believe that the MediaBridge technology will play a crucial enabling role in the future of e-commerce. By allowing consumers to quickly and easily find more information about products and services that are of interest to them, it will facilitate the growth of marketing over the web and the growth of Internet retailing.

Video Piracy Prevention

"The International Intellectual Property Alliance estimates that U.S. copyright industries lost at least $12.4 billion worldwide due to copyright piracy in 1998," (Prospectus, p. 33) and without preventative measures these losses will only increase, as image technology continues to become cheaper and more powerful. Some time back, the motion picture industry, represented by most of the major studios and the Motion Picture Association of America, formed a working group to identify a standard for DVD security which would likely focus on digital watermarking. In July 2000 the Millennium Group announced a combined digital watermarking and play-control system for DVD recorders and PC devices. The system enables playback devices to identify illegally copied discs and prevent copying or playback of illegal copies. It will also provide a copy-once watermark re-marking technology for applications in which one copy of a video is allowed.

Secure Documents

In Congressional testimony, the U.S. Treasury identified an alarming increase in counterfeiting activity that is being driven by high-resolution scanners and printers. The Treasury Department estimated that 43% of all counterfeit bank notes seized in 1998 were produced with personal computers, as compared to only 0.5% in 1995. Also, the amount of U.S. counterfeit bank notes increased over 30% in the twelve months ended September 1998. Digimarc's existing relationship with several leading central banks gives the company a jump on dominating the rapidly developing digital counterfeit-prevention market. There are numerous other applications for Digimarc's technology in this area, such as protecting financial instruments, stocks, bonds, identity documents such as passports, and even tickets for sporting events. Recently, there has been growing concern about the production of fraudulent tickets. "Organizers of the World Cup and Super Bowl recently adopted currency and check security techniques that required costly design and printing alterations."

(Prospectus, p. 34) The potential applications for Digimarc's digital watermark seem almost unlimited.

Competition

Digimarc does face significant competition in some of its markets. Most notably, in the paper-as-portal arena the company faces an alliance between Motorola and Symbol Technologies, among others. Digimarc is well positioned to compete with these challengers, but it is still a little too early to try and predict a clear winner. We believe that one of the company's primary strengths is that it is relying on an open architecture to deliver its service. Many of the competing technologies require special readers to access the web-based on printed material. MediaBridge, however, will work with most scanners already on the market and with a number of leading PC cameras. Furthermore, the Motorola/Symbol venture will require their customers to register each web code with the vendor, while Digimarc's clients will be able to assign their own codes. However, in the area of using digital watermarks to protect currency, we are not aware of any significant competition for Digimarc. Given that the company currently sports a market capitalization of less than $300 million and has $140 million in cash and no long-term debt, we believe that the potential for generating licensing revenue from the currency watermarking alone could justify the current market cap.

Partners and Alliances

Digimarc has well-established alliances with several leading technology firms and continues to seek opportunities for developing new markets through innovative applications of its digital watermarking technology. In the Millennium Group, the company has partnered with Macrovision and Philips to use digital rights-management techniques to deter the counterfeiting of DVD disks. On September 18, 2000, Royal Philips Electronics invested and Macrovision increased its existing stake in DMRC at a price of $20 per share (at a time when the company's stock was trading at approximately $14 per share). After accounting for this most recent round of investments, Philips and Macrovision both own approximately 12% of Digimarc.

The company also recently announced a new alliance with Pitney Bowes, which will use DMRC's digital watermarking technology for metered mail. The two companies will work together to develop new ways to use the watermark as a security feature for metered postage (Pitney Bowes offers the ClickStamp Internet postage solution). The digital watermark could facilitate the issuance of stamps over the Internet by helping curb counterfeiting.

The watermark could also provide an instantaneous link to a specific web site. For instance, a credit card company could include the watermark in a bill, which would then send its customers to a site containing information on their account (or special offers).

We are impressed by Digimarc's ingenuity in seeking new markets for its technology, but even more important is the company's willingness to seek partners to help it capitalize on its opportunities. The expertise and financial strength of Digimarc's partners will play a crucial role as the company seeks to extend its reach in competitive markets.

Conclusion

Digimarc is already well positioned to dominate the counterfeit and piracy prevention markets and the company has the resources and applications in place to be a top player in the move towards paper-as-portal marketing. Digimarc has already taken the necessary steps to protect its own intellectual property with a broad patent portfolio that should yield significant, high-margin licensing revenue for years to come. The company also has established relationships with a number of leading technology firms, and it has the financial strength and financial backing necessary to develop its potential long-term.

Digimarc Corporation
NASDAQ Symbol: DMRC
19801 SW 72nd Ave. Suite 250
Tualatin, OR 97062
1-503-885-9699
1-800-DIGIMARC
CEO Bruce Davis
Web Site www.digimarc.com

Undersea
Fiber-Optic Network
Global Crossing

Global Fiber-Optic Network

In days past, we pushed a pen or pencil across a piece of paper in order to exchange ideas and information; today, we push light through tens of thousands of miles of glass to exchange data worldwide. This is the present and future of telecommunications. In order to understand the future, let us take a look at the past.

It all started by a seed of ingenuity planted more than 120 years ago by an immigrant to the United States. Believe it or not, the first use of light as a carrier of information was in the design and working prototype of a photo-phone (light phone) invented by Alexander Graham Bell in 1880. Bell invented a device where he could speak into a microphone, which in turn would vibrate a mirror. This mirror would reflect sunlight to a receiving mirror approximately 650 feet away. The mirror on the receiver would cause a selenium crystal to vibrate, and sound would be generated at the other end. This photo-phone would allow people to communicate over open spaces. However, there was one major drawback: if there were no sunlight, there was no transmission path. So it didn't work on rainy days, after sunset, or if a passing animal or person blocked the signal. Due to this drawback, and other pressing inventions, Alexander moved on to different things. However, Mr. Bell was quoted as saying, "This is THE greatest invention I have ever made; greater than the telephone." The photo-phone was the precursor, using those same principles, for the development of today's light-based communication systems and networks. Instead of sunlight, we are using invisible laser light and blasting it through a fine glass cable. Now, we don't have to worry about nightfall, a rainy day, or other interruptions to our sunlight-enabled "data path," we generate our own light, and are no longer limited to the original 650-feet distance limitation.

Over the past 100 years or so, we have used copper cable to send electrical signals of communication to each other and from one continent to the other. This worked, and is still working, but with limitations. Imagine the existing copper cables to be a small water pipe. Only so much water can get through that size of pipe. The larger the pipe the more "water" or data can be passed through it. In the 1960s the use of satellite began, which was an even bigger "pipe." However, today there is an even larger pipe in use and an ever-expanding network that has caused a paradigm shift in telecommunications.

In today's world, in the time it takes a person to take a marble and drop it from his hand to the floor, well over 1.6 *trillions* bits of data, (or the entire contents of the United States Library of Congress in a matter of seconds) could be sent through glass fiber from the United States to Europe. Thanks to this expanded and ever-increasing data pipe, information IS moving at the speed of light. Utilizing fiber-optic cables and networks, on land (terrestrial), and under the sea (suboceanic), we are able to move immense amounts of data around the globe at literally the blink of an eye. Never before in the history of mankind have we been able to move such vast amounts of information across such vast spaces in fractions of a second.

How is this done? By using pure, tiny glass filaments and pump lasers, a wavelength of light encoded with data is sent through a fiber-optic strand to a receiver at the other end. This fiber-optic strand is as thin as a human hair, but with a clarity never before imagined. One source we researched states that there are companies currently manufacturing fiber-optic cable so pure that if it were a wall of glass seventy miles thick, one could see through it to the other side. The amount of data that can be pushed through this fiber "pipe" is only limited to the number of pipes available and the spectrum of laser light generated. Scientists are now working on breaking the existing laser down into various spectrums or "colors" and then encoding these unique wavelengths with their own data, thus enabling multiple channels of information to be pushed through one fiber.

Fiber-optic networks are currently in place and continue to be installed all over the world. Installation and network infrastructure companies are planning ahead and installing an overabundance of fiber that is not even being used, knowing full well that in the future it will be tapped. This unused fiber is known as "dark fiber." This fiber is called dark because it is laying there unused, untapped, just waiting to be energized with a beam of laser light.

The use for this fiber network is limited only to the imagination. The explosion of bandwidth will facilitate live-streaming high-quality video, audio, and the movement of massive amounts of data. It will bring about uses that we haven't even imagined yet. This network is bringing to us what is called "broadband," or very large bandwidth. These broadband services are now being used in business, education, and personal lives throughout the world.

In doing a search on the Internet today, the request and its reply will more than likely pass through an existing fiber-optic cable. The financial, investment, and worldwide banking sectors have already jumped on this technology. This network, or backbone of the Internet, is providing a "data-bahn" on which one day, in the very near future, the majority of people will traverse on a wave of, and at the speed of, light.

Back to the copper cables mentioned previously. We have existing suboceanic cables connecting the continents. They are slow compared to what fiber-optics can do, expensive, and increasingly becoming obsolete. It is time that the digital plumbing be reworked to make way for the exploding evolution of broadband communications.

There is a missing link in this plan. What company has the foresight and initiative to bring about this change and supply the need for global terrestrial and suboceanic fiber connectivity? Who is a key player providing the conduit for all this movement of data to take place?

That company is Global Crossing. Global Crossing provides sophisticated managed data and voice products and services to large users of international bandwidth, such as multinational corporations, governments and ISPs, and more importantly, Internet functionality. Long distance is a very small portion of their business. It is undertaking one of the largest projects of laying fiber-optic cables across the bottom of the sea. Not only is it providing and installing "transoceanic" fiber cables, but the company is combining this with their existing and ever expanding terrestrial fiber-optic networks. Global Crossing is creating one of largest Internet Protocol based fiber-optic networks in the world. No other company we know of at the time of this printing is undertaking such a behemoth project.

According to our research, Global Crossing is connecting five continents, twenty-seven countries, and more than two hundred major cities. In essence, it is creating a new fiber web, which will offer connectivity to leading business centers worldwide at mind-boggling speeds. This connectivity will bring together continents, nations, cities, and ultimately, desktops around the world.

Global Crossing
You Can Bridge an Ocean with a Glass Cable

There has been an explosion of bandwidth creation in the United States intended to handle the surging demands of data transmission, wireless communications and bandwidth-hungry applications, such as videoconferencing. At the same time, Internet use and telecommunications demand has been growing dramatically overseas creating an ever-increasing demand for international communication capacity. Global Crossing's undersea fiber-optic cables are well positioned to help meet that demand. The company may someday be the leading provider of intercontinental data communications services.

Company Description

Global Crossing, based in Hamilton, Bermuda, has one of the most extensive private networks of undersea fiber-optic cable, which is complemented by its sizable terrestrial fiber systems. The company's fiber-optic cables already cross the Atlantic and Pacific Oceans and attach to its network of terrestrial cable linking major cities in the U.S., Europe, Japan, and Latin America. Global Crossing is still expanding its network as well as developing an array of scalable services for its retail customers. The company provides Internet and other data services such as videoconferencing as well as long-distance telecommunications services. Global Crossing also operates at the wholesale level by leasing capacity to major international carriers.

When completed, the Global Crossing Network will encompass 101,000 route miles and will serve over two hundred major cities in twenty-seven countries (expected completion date is mid-2001). The company expects to address approximately 80% of the world's international communications traffic. What is truly unique about Global Crossing, however, is the strategic positioning of its fiber-optic capacity. As discussed by George Gilder in his book *Telecosm*, "underseas bandwidth is currently under 1 percent of terrestrial bandwidth and is increasing only 4 percent as fast…with the growth in the number of foreign Internet users rapidly outpacing U.S. growth, undersea traffic will grow several times faster than terrestrial traffic. Over the next five years, the submarine portions of the Internet will prove to be an agonizing chokepoint." (p. 276) It is interesting to note that Global Crossing also owns the largest fleet of cable-laying and maintenance vessels in the world (Global Marine Systems) and currently services more than a third of the world's undersea cable miles. (www.globalcrossing.com) Global Crossing hasn't stopped at simply supplying the backbone for telecommunications but actually provides a comprehensive set of scalable services for both wholesale and retail clients. Some of the company's value-added services include Virtual Private Networks (VPNs), other managed services and teleconferencing or videoconferencing services.

Company History

Global Crossing began constructing its undersea links in 1997 and initiated service between London and New York in May 1998. The company went public in August 1998 at $9.50 per share split-adjusted. In July 1999, Global Crossing began a series of acquisitions that dramatically enhanced the scope of its business. The company purchased Global Marine Systems (July 1999), Frontier Corp., which included the web-hosting business eventually called GlobalCenter (September 1999), Racal Telecom (November 1999), a 50% interest in the Hutchison Global Crossing joint venture (completed January 2000) and IPC communications and IXnet (June 2000). Even though the company has grown explosively and completed a string of acquisitions, it appears to still have a very clear focus on its primary goal of providing first-class international communication.

Global Crossing has repeatedly demonstrated its commitment to focusing on international communications. In June 2000, Global Crossing announced the sale of its incumbent local-exchange carrier operations for $3.65 billion in cash (at a gain of over $1 billion over carrying value). The sale of the slower-growth local business results in a more focused and leaner operation. Furthermore, the company recently announced the sale of its web-hosting business to Exodus Communications for over $6 billion in stock, which will result in Global Crossing holding an approximately 17% in Exodus and a seat on the board. Additionally, Exodus signed a ten-year network services agreement stating that it will purchase 50% or more of its future network needs outside of Asia from Global Crossing (the value of these services is estimated at over $4 billion). Exodus and Global Crossing also agreed to combine their web-hosting assets in Asia into a joint venture which will be 33% owned by Asia Global Crossing. This joint venture has the stated intention that it will purchase 67% or more of its network needs from Asia Global Crossing. The sale of these non-core assets will help finance the buildout of the remainder of Global Crossing's system.

Global Crossing already has a substantial network in place and is progressing towards its vision of a globally integrated all-fiber network. Atlantic Crossing 1 already connects America and Europe, and the company has existing networks that provide connections to over 50 major cities in the U.S. and Europe. Global Crossing is dramatically expanding its network and will soon incorporate the leading urban centers in Latin America and Asia. Ground lines will be built linking urban centers in South America and a north-south system will connect North America to Mexico, Latin America and the rest of the Western Hemisphere. On August 31, 2000, the company announced the shore landing of its South American Crossing cable at Rio de Janeiro. AT&T Latin America has already signed on for over $40 million of high-speed capacity from Global Crossing. In Asia, the company plans to connect Hutchison Global Crossing's existing terrestrial fiber-optic network in Hong Kong with Japan by 2000 and then Taiwan and Korea by the first half of 2001. The existing link between Japan and California (Pacific Crossing 1) will connect Asia to the company's global network.

We believe that the positioning of Global Crossing's assets is the key to the story, but some may question the turnover in top management at the company. Leo Hindery, the former CEO, left after only seven months at the helm. His primary goal seems to have been to engineer the sale of GlobalCenter on a favorable basis, which has already been accomplished. Thomas Casey, Global Crossing's new CEO, brings a variety of telecommunications experience to the table. He has been with the company since 1998 and has served as Vice Chairman and director. Prior to joining Global Crossing, Mr. Casey was co-head of the Global Communications Investment Banking Group at Merrill Lynch for three years. Mr. Casey also was co-head of the telecommunications and media group of the law firm of Skadden, Arps, Slate, Meagher and Flom from 1990 to 1995. He also spent six years as a lawyer for the federal government working at the FCC and in the Department of Justice's Antitrust Division.

Why is there a Need for Global Crossing's Technology?

There are numerous contributing factors as to why Global Crossing's technology is both uniquely important and timely, but the overwhelming determinant is on the demand side: the rise of the Internet outside the U.S. borders is creating a true Global Village and will contribute to dramatically increased demand for intercontinental communication. Internet usage outside the U.S. has been growing explosively, but there are still numerous areas where penetration is low. Global Reach estimates that there will be 206 million Internet users in 2000 but this figure is expected to more than triple to 621 million by 2003 with the most rapid growth occurring outside of the U.S. As a result of the surge in Internet use overseas, we expect to see dramatic increases in international telecommunications traffic over the next decade. Also, there is currently only a limited amount of fiber-optic capacity linking between the continents where Global Crossing is currently a dominant player. The factor, which sets Global Crossing apart in terms of its service to the end-user, is its seamless international network. Generally, to connect from a major European city to Tokyo, a telecommunications customer must access one system in Europe, make a connection to a trans-Atlantic cable, and contract with a telco in the U.S. to cross North America before making the final link to Japan. Global Crossing can offer the same customer significantly quicker access through its internal network without having to shift the call to any other carrier.

Partners and Alliances

In order to accelerate the completion of its network, Global Crossing has taken advantage of opportunities to forge partnerships with leading companies in developing its Asian links. The company has developed a joint venture with Hutchison Whampoa, Hutchison Global Crossing, which has established a terrestrial fiber network in Hong Kong. Asia Global Crossing (which is now traded separately on the NASDAQ while Global Crossing retains a 57% interest) was developed jointly with Microsoft and Softbank to provide broadband telecommunications services in Japan and Southeast Asia. The plan is for the system to eventually link Taiwan, Singapore, Malaysia, Korea, the Philippines and if regulations permit, China, with the existing operations in Hong Kong and Japan. Global Crossing is also making use of partnerships to offer value-added services to its clients. The company offers videoconferencing with collaboration, which allows users to share applications and presentations by using WebEx's technology. The company recently decided to sell its web-hosting operations to Exodus Communications, but the two will actually still be coordinating on several fronts. Global Crossing will offer a web-hosting service that is cobranded with Exodus to its customers. Also, Asia Global Crossing and Exodus have formed a joint venture to provide web-hosting which will be 33% owned by Asia Global Crossing.

Conclusion

Global Crossing's intercontinental fiber-optic links provide what will prove to be a critical missing piece of the puzzle as the Global Village truly begins to take shape. We believe that demand for international communications will grow exponentially over the next decade and that the company will be a prime enabler of this trend as it provides a seamless, one-stop shop for customers seeking true global communications capability.

Global Crossing
NASDAQ Symbol: GX
360 North Crescent Drive
Beverly Hills, CA 90210
CEO Thomas Casey
Web Site www.globalcrossing.com

Photonic Switching

Avanex

"Powering the Next Generation Optical Networks—Today, and Progressing at the Speed of Light"

Photonics

When one walks into a dark room and flip a switch that turns on a light, what happens? The thin filament within that light bulb is energized with electricity and floods the room with photons. (Let there be light!) Photons—"the quantum of electromagnetic energy, generally regarded as a discrete particle having *zero* mass, *no* electric charge, and an *indefinitely* long lifetime." (*The American Heritage Dictionary of the English Language, Third Edition*, Houghton Mifflin, 1996) These particles race wildly and uncontrollably around the room instantaneously, bouncing off items and reflecting back to the human eye the photons that were not absorbed, thus given the perception of what we know as color. That is until those particles hit something black, whereupon they are as mysteriously absorbed into nothingness as they were generated in the first place. To understand photons is to understand where we are today with the explosion of the Internet. By using and controlling photons we are enabling our computers to connect, communicate, and share data through the Internet. Since photons act so wildly, how are they controlled and transmitted? Wrangling photons is like herding cats!

In 1957, the way we created and handled them changed. With a new and revolutionary invention of Gordon Gould, we were able to take uncontrollable photons and focus them into a coherent beam of light.

Light Amplification by Stimulated Emission of Radiation...the laser was born! Problem solved, right? In part, yes. After that, in 1963 at the ITT Labs of London, Charles K. Kao, a then-thirty-year-old scientist from Shanghai, hypothesized and finally proved that photons could not only be wrangled, but also used to transmit near-limitless amounts of data via pulses of that same laser light. He went on to prove that these pulses of light can be sent through strands of glass fiber not much larger than the human hair. Due to the insight and persistence of Kao, who is now known as "the father of fiber optics," we are now ushering in the age of worldwide fiber-optic-enabled communications and witnessing the explosion of the photonics industry.

Now, let's take a look at photonics. Photons, Dense Wavelength Division Multiplexing (DWDM), silicon nanocrystals, optical amplifiers, photonic band-gap crystals, pump lasers, lambdas, and fiber optics. Do these terms sound like part of a dialogue from a science-fiction movie? They are now commonplace terms in technical circles and slowly migrating their way into more mainstream speech. What does the word "photonics" bring to mind? Many might scratch their heads and say, "Huh?" Alternatively, some might be so astounded at what we are saying here, that they shake their heads in disbelief. If so, that reaction wouldn't be far off the mark with how most of society views, or knows about, photonics. "Photonics is the science and technology based on and concerned with the controlled flow of photons, or light particles. It is the optical equivalent of electronics, and the two technologies coexist in such innovations as opto-electronic integrated circuits. Photonic applications include data storage (using optical disks and holograms), data transmission (see fiber optics), experimental optical computers, optical switches and light modulators (for signal processing and interconnection.)" (*The Concise Columbia Electronic Encyclopedia*, 1999) It seems what we are doing with light, and the technology thereof, is as foreign to the general population as what electricity was to people back in the late 1800s. When looking at the whole sector of photonics, it smacks of futuristic science fiction. But, whether one thinks it is science fiction or not, photonics is an integral part of today's world.

Is photonics a new thing? No, not really. Scientists have been studying light and its properties for centuries. But not until the 20th century have there been any major advances. Thanks in part to Charles K. Kao and many of his peers throughout the world, we are able to harness the power of light and incorporate what we know of this science for various commercial, personal, and medical applications. Most people don't even realize it when they have brushes with photonics. When they play a CD while driving or at home, photonics technology is used. Snapping a picture using a new digital camera, photonics. Go in for vision corrective surgery using lasers, again photonics. Make a phone call across the United States or overseas, and chances are a beam of light is carrying one's voice. Researching on the Internet, looking at a web site, watching a streaming video, or participating in a live global e-conference—all possible in part by photonics.

In this chapter we will focus on this last application of photonics-broadband delivery through the Internet. Utilizing this ever evolving and innovative science in the application of data delivery and telecommunication we are creating one of the most sophisticated global webs of light.

Using lasers and ultra-thin threads of glass, scientists are able to take light, concentrate it into a pure beam (Lambdas), and have it act as a transport via pulses to carry information. They are sending this laser light through glass strands that are four times the thickness of a human hair, or 125 microns, and have a degree of clarity and purity never before imagined. Technology exists today to take those light waves, break them down into "channels" (or colors) and pass at least forty separate channels through one glass fiber, with one channel having the capacity to service all the data needs of one small city. It's having an incredible social and economic impact on our society today. It allows us to communicate, collaborate, share data, voice, and video faster and more economically. It is generating new businesses and creating jobs. Using this technology as a supporting backbone of the Internet, it is ushering in the era of broadband, ultra high-speed communications and commerce. In its current form, it is marrying the computer, which is electronic, with fiber optics, a light-powered technology. It is about connectivity, reliability, and quality of service. All of which fiber optics and the surrounding technology will deliver! Today's estimate of the fiber market alone is more than $10 billion and is expected to reach over $40 billion within the next three years. With today's advances in this technology, and the spin-offs it is creating, it is forming a worldwide multi-trillion dollar market.

Avanex: Company Description

Avanex Corporation (AVNX) based in Freemont, California, designs and manufactures a small yet attractive line of high-quality, high-performance, fiber-optics-based products known as photonic processors. These devices enable communication companies to increase the performance and capacity of their existing optical networks. At the same time it's providing those same companies increased cost-effectiveness, increased miniaturization and a reduction in the complexity typically inherent in today's new fiber-optics networks. This is Avanex's mission and it is well on the way to accomplishing it, which is no small feat with the recent explosive growth of the photonics industry.

Avanex currently has a total of sixty patents (pending and issued). One of the company's crowning jewels to date was issued on October 10, 2000, when it was awarded a patent for a proprietary DWDM process. Patent #6,130,971 is a "Fiber Optic Dense Wavelength Division Multiplexer with a Phase Differential Method of Wavelength Separation Utilizing a Polarization Beam Splitter and a Nonlinear Interferometer." Avanex's current Chief Technology Officer, Dr. Simon Cao, invented this process. It enables the splitting of an optical signal into an extraordinarily high number of wavelengths, each capable of carrying a unique stream of data. Avanex has achieved 1,000 wavelengths in laboratory experiments, whereas the current commercial maximum is 160 wavelengths. It also can be easily modified to allow channels to be dropped or added, which has been a major problem for an all-optical communications network. This latest patent issue was significant for Avanex in that it protects valuable intellectual property and establishes a formidable competitive barrier! The company's PowerMux product is based on the patented DWDM process and is being shipped commercially.

Company History

Avanex was incorporated in 1997 and has rapidly established itself as a force in the photonics industry. Quarterly revenues for the company were $34.8 million for the quarter ended September 29, 2000, up from just over $500,000 in the June quarter of 1999. Avanex has invested heavily for the future as it seeks to capitalize on its innovative technology. Since June of 1999, the company's head count has increased from 60 employees to over 1,100, which includes 180 Research and Development Engineers (a strong R&D effort will be critical for staying on the cutting edge of the photonics industry). Over the same time period, Avanex has increased its customer base from five to over ten major players in the industry. Avanex's key customers include: Cisco (CSCO), Hitachi (HIT), MCI WorldCom (WCOM), Fujitsu (FJTSY), Nortel (NT), and Sycamore (SCMR). The company has over 362,000 square feet of manufacturing space—287,000 square feet in the United States and approximately 75,000 of contracted manufacturing space in Tianjin, China.

Avanex has an impressive and highly experienced management team and board of directors. Leading as Chairman and Chief Executive Officer is Dr. Walter Alessandrini, who has been with the company since March 1999. Prior to his current position, he was President and Chief Executive Officer of Pirelli Cables and Systems, North America Division (a division with 1,400 employees and sales of nearly $750 million). Before that, he was President and CEO of Union Switch and Signal. He earned his doctorate degree in Mechanical Engineering from the University of Genoa, Italy. Jessy Chao serves as the CFO and was one of Avanex's founders. Before he co-founded Avanex, he served as the Director of Finance and Business Operations at E-TEK Dynamics, Inc.

Paul Engle, President and COO, joined the company in 2000 after helping oversee the successful spin-off of Agilent Technologies from Hewlett Packard in November 1999. Mr. Engle joined Hewlett Packard in 1993 as General Manager of the Fiber Optic Components Operation. In February 1997, he assumed full profit and loss responsibility for H-P's worldwide fiber-optics component business, which grew to be one of the world's largest before being spun-off in 1999.

The rest of the Avanex Management Team is comprised of Dr. Simon Cao, Chief Technology Officer, formerly with Oplink and E-TEK Dynamics; Giovanni Barbarossa, Product Development, formerly with Lucent and Agilent; Dr. Charles Mao, V.P. of Product Marketing and Application Strategy, formerly with WorldCom; Peter Maguire, V.P of Worldwide Sales, formerly with Pirelli and Fujitsu; Paul Jiang,

Manufacturing, formerly with E-Tek Dynamics; James Pickering, Quality Control, formerly with ETEC Systems; Brett Casebolt, Business Development, formerly with Morgan Stanley; and Tony Florence, Corporate Marketing, formerly with Ansaldo Signal. Avanex's Board of Directors hails from companies such as MCI WorldCom, Synaptics, Brocade, Bank of America, Mayfield Funds, Sequoia Capital, and Crosspoint Venture.

Why is there such a need for their products?

As we all know, traffic on the Internet is growing exponentially. By some estimates the volume will triple each year for the next several years. As people use the Internet more and demand richer, more graphically intensive content the traffic will overwhelm our existing telecommunications networks. Bandwidth is being choked and limited by the existing cables, switches, and routers. We are trying to ram more data through those same networks and placing a tremendous burden on them. Some people believe throwing more fiber at the problem will make it go away. It does help, but installing new fiber is a very expensive undertaking. We need a way to increase bandwidth and get more out of our existing network infrastructure.

When it comes to generating light signals (optical packets of information) and passing them through a fiber-optic cable, it's not a hard task to perform. The difficult part comes when one actually tries to process or do something with those signals. Adding, dropping, and switching them in real time without the use of extensive electronic means is one of the major hurdles this industry faces. The less an optical packet has to be switched via an electronic-conversion process the better. When the packets remain in the form of light and are not converted to electronic packets, they move faster, more efficiently, and with lower signal loss over a network. Compounding that basic problem is again the exploding demand for bandwidth that is clogging our existing telecommunications networks. Again, we need a way to push more data through our existing infrastructure. Avanex is designing and supplying devices that are addressing that need and making it easier and more cost effective to switch and process these optical packets. The good thing about the company's photonic processors is that they enable high bit-rate transmissions on any type of fiber and, at the same time, allow a cost-effective way to migrate to the next-generation networks that are coming our way.

Primary Products

The leading product of Avanex is the PowerMux, which is a DWDM (Dense Wavelength Division Multiplexer) device. What is a multiplexer? An optical multiplexer is a device that can take many different wavelengths (packets) of light that are carrying information at the same time and send those various wavelengths together through the same single strand of fiber-optic cable. This device allows those wavelengths to be "muxed" and "demuxed," that is, it puts all the wavelengths together, sends them through a single fiber (multiplex), and then separates them back out (demultiplex) when they arrive at their destination through the optical network. Avanex's multiplexers have demonstrated handling 800 channels at a transmission rate of up to three terabits of data per second over a single fiber. By the way, one terabit of data equals one trillion bits of data; that's 1,000,000,000,000! The PowerMux NxG is the second generation of the PowerMux device, which will be available during the first quarter of 2001. It provides greater performance and ultimately a lower cost, using a relatively new technology the company obtained through a recent acquisition of Holographix Corporation. This increase in performance translates into lower cost per wavelength transmitted. The current average manufacturing cost per wavelength is about $500. Avanex's product can lower that cost to about $100 per wavelength.

The PowerFilter products are wavelength separators that are used to "read" incoming light signals as part of the WDM process. The problem with earlier optical filters is that they lose a lot of the signal as they pass through the filtering process in a conventional multiplexer. The PowerFilter has corrected much of this problem, reducing the loss and increasing transmission distances. They improve the overall performance and at the same time reduce the cost, since system operators will need to use fewer of these filters. The PowerFilter Band Separators can isolate and separate out up to four wavelengths per unit, which also reduces the number of filters needed.

The PowerExchanger is an add/drop processor, which allows any number of channels (packets of information) to be added to or dropped from the main line of a fiber-optic network (trunk) at any destination as they travel through the network. It operates in a switchless environment while offering real-time configuration of all optical add/drop muxing. It is like an on/off ramp for the information superhighway. It utilizes a combination of the PowerMux multiplexing and demultiplexing photonic processors along with Avanex's proprietary Electro-strictive, Electro-optic, and Magneto-optic technology that enables photonic redirection of signals. Since this redirection happens in the optical domain, the signal quality is maintained from point-to-point and at any point in between. It is considered "switchless" since the packets don't have to be converted into an electronic signal (which is expensive and inefficient), then switched or routed, and then converted back into light to continue on its way to its final destination.

The PowerShaper processors have been designed to correct bandwidth and distance limitations in the transmission of signals over today's fiber. They restore the integrity of the light signals, allowing those signals to be transmitted over longer distances without electrically aided regeneration, which again slows the process down and is expensive. The PowerShaper also prevents signals from mixing and corrupting the transmission of data over greater distances.

And the last product they manufacture is the PowerExpress Integrated Long-Haul Processor. This is a next-generation 2R (Regenerate and Reshape) Optical Line Amplifier for DWDM systems. It amplifies channels and offers higher output power for the optical packets.

Competition

Avanex's major competition comes from JDS Uniphase/SDL (JDSU), Corning (GLW), and Oplink (OPLK). These companies also produce multiplexers, filters, and other sub-system processors, but the solutions they provide are considered reactionary in nature whereas Avanex uses what it terms a "push-pull" model. The push-pull model is more customized for each client. Using this model, they design their optical product based on what the carrier needs and wants and then build the solution exclusively for them or their systems integrator. No piecemeal systems here! What impressed us the most was the fact that Avanex focuses on designing and building next-generation systems. It is one of the only companies who can manufacture 100 channel DWDMs in volume. The company integrates its PowerMux line of multiplexers to accomplish this.

Conclusion

We believe that Avanex is the up-and-coming industry leader in photonic sub-system processor design and manufacturing. With its products, it is enabling existing optic network systems to be improved and easily migrated to the next generation of fiber-optic networks. It has the potential to be a leader in this sector within the next five years. Avanex is positioned to do for the next generation of global fiber-optic networks what the microchip did for today's computers.

Avanex
NASDAQ Symbol: AVNX
40919 Encyclopedia Circle
Fremont, CA 94538, USA
510-897-4188
CEO Walter Alessandrini
Web Site www.avanex.com

Internet Infrastructure Service—Search

Inktomi Corp.
Enhancing Internet Efficiency
Through Innovative Infrastructure

Internet Infrastructure Service (IIS)—Portal Platforms

"The Internet is a wondrous thing." What a simple statement about such a complex entity! Because of the Internet, information is now just a keystroke, mouse click, verbal command, or stylus tap away. From our computers, cell phones, and PDAs, people have an ever-increasing fount of knowledge on which to draw.

Sector History

In the new millennium, people worldwide are poised and ready to draw from that well of knowledge. However, the challenge today is to get the desired content and information in a way that serves our individual needs best. Not too long ago, getting information off the Internet was a tedious process. One would execute an Internet search, which was difficult and confusing without knowing the proper syntax, and receive a search return that, more times than not, contained unwanted information. Then one would have to sift through those results, making for a time-consuming process. Plus one didn't know which site to go to get the needed information. We needed "intelligent buckets" and a few all-encompassing user-friendly wells! We now have them, and they are called portals.

Structure of this Industry

The Internet of today is composed of millions of computers net-worked together worldwide to provide the services and information we've grown to expect. In order for this to work, there must be a struc-ture holding it all together. Everyone—be it single, corporate user or network provider—has to connect using specified standards, protocol, and equipment. Otherwise, it would be close to impossible to work together and share data and services in a productive and expeditious manner. Everything we use that supports the flow and processing of our information is what we call the Internet Infrastructure. This includes all the specialized software and hardware used for maintenance, support, and service in keeping the web working—enabling us individually to get the information we need. In this sector, we will focus on specific Internet Infrastructure Services and in some cases, hardware that works within this Infrastructure, but more importantly improves the quality of our Internet experience. We will explore a company that provides enhanced search engine software, and one that provides tools to make portals more powerful.

What is a Portal?

A portal is a "point of entry" to the World Wide Web and serves up a broad assortment of resources and services, such as e-mail, chat forums, search engines, and on-line shopping. It allows the user an easy way to search and utilize various services on the site. It is intended to be the first place people go to when they are using the web. A portal will have an easy-to-use search engine and a catalog of links to other web sites and services. The first web portals were made up of dial-up on-line services, like America Online, that provided web access in addition to their one-stop resources. Today, there are search-engine sites that have transformed themselves into portals. By doing this, they have the potential to attract and keep a larger number of web visitors. People will go there for convenience and ease of use and will keep coming back time and time again.

The majority of portals today are accessed via computer. But the new portals of today, and the ever-expanding portals of tomorrow, are acces-sible through Wireless Application Protocol (WAP) enabled cell phones, personal digital assistants, two-way pagers, screen telephones and television set-top boxes. This obviously will give the user more flexibility and convenience. It is enabling the delivery of a wide variety of services to the consumer and merchant. The advantages to the consumer are enormous. From one easy-to-use device, be it a computer, PDA or cell phone, it allows the user to locate a merchant, local or otherwise, and one would be able to comparison shop, receive promotions, take discounts, and make purchases all with a single click or tap. It will also allow communications such as chat-room dialog and instant messaging, and personal services such as address book, calendar, and to-do list administration. Merchants, on the other hand, have the ability to leverage the portal service so they can design and create an on-line presence, advertise their services and products, and allow those services and products to be purchased effortlessly by the consumer. It will allow the merchant to target his product directly to specific consumers.

How is all this possible? This is where the Internet Infrastructure Service (IIS) providers come in. These companies have scalable software, server network and cross-platform solutions that enable other companies to leverage the portal's powerful services. A cross-platform solution is one that allows multiple and various users the same access to the information being served, regardless of what device they are using, be it a PDA, cell phone, or computer. Web site designers utilizing these services of the IIS providers are building some of the most user-friendly, content-rich sites with powerful search-engine capabilities. The majority of search engines used today on web sites are in fact powered by just a few back-end IIS providers' software and systems.

Market potential

With the explosive growth of the Internet and wireless Internet access, it's difficult, if not impossible, to predict with any accuracy the potential market for Internet Infrastructure Services. The Wireless Portal Services sector alone is forecasted to reach in excess of $40 billion by 2005. Everyday, these companies seem to come up with a new application for their portal services. The growth potential is huge.

How is this sector changing the world?

With the use of the Internet growing exponentially every month, we are just now seeing the potential of what good Internet Infrastructure Service providers can do. This sector is still in its infancy, but the impact it's having is already world-changing.

Future of the sector

It is wonderful to think that consumers will have, at their fingertips, all the information and services the Internet has to offer, in an easy-to-use format. Whether it's research, communications, or shopping, people will be able to find and get what they want, when they want it and how they want it. Merchants will be able to increase awareness of their products, sales, and customer base. They will be able to advertise to a target group of potential clients, thus increasing the efficacy of their advertising dollars.

Conclusion

The Internet Infrastructure Service providers are working together with the leading web site portals and cellular communications companies, throughout the world, who are building the next generation of super portals. Two of the companies that are leading the way are Inktomi and InfoSpace.

Inktomi

"We want to become the operating system of the Internet."
—David Peterschmidt, Inktomi CEO

A rather simple statement on its face, but a very lofty goal. Before dismissing this goal out of hand, consider that this Internet infrastructure company already powers the lion's share of the Internet's leading search engines and currently commands over 50% of the carrier-class caching market. Inktomi develops and markets scalable applications that are core to the Internet infrastructure, enabling end users to easily find information and access it more quickly. Inktomi's software is designed for use by global enterprises, media companies, and service providers in the

Internet access, backbone, broadband, hosting, and content markets. Inktomi continually adds best of class services to its Internet infrastructure platform to provide a customer-oriented solution that is seamless, scalable to their needs, and as efficient as possible.

Company Description

Chances are that when any given search engine is accessed, the software that powers it was not provided by the company that operates the portal being used. Most portals rely on other companies to provide the infrastructure software, which actually powers their search engines. The Internet is so incredibly complex and diverse that no one company can dominate it in the same way that IBM used to dominate mainframe computing or the way that Microsoft gained hegemony over the PC for corporate applications. In fact, what truly makes the Internet unique is that there are almost no barriers to entry. Even a teenager with relatively little experience and limited resources can set up a web page and publish or show pictures on it. How then can an Internet company develop the kind of sustained competitive advantage that is required to justify a large stock market capitalization and even drive it higher? The evidence seems to be conclusive that simply trying to sell goods over the web is not really a sustainable advantage. So besides selling computer hardware, what is a way for a company to play a dramatic role in the spread of the Internet and develop some kind of a sustainable advantage? Inktomi provides the role-model example to answer that question. Kevin Ryan, the CFO of DoubleClick was asked, "What [Internet] company can possibly justify its valuation?" Without hesitation, he answered, "Inktomi." (*Greenmagazine*, Ken Kurson, April 2000, p. 1)

Inktomi provides the search technology that drives more than 120 portals and destination sites, including a number of the web's leaders like the search function found in AOL. In fact, the company has won a number of awards for its search technology (see table) from *PC Magazine* and other leading technology journals.

Inktomi also dominates the carrier-class caching market (which means general Internet usage such as using an Internet Service Provider). However, what is truly impressive is that this dominant position in caching enables Inktomi's software to become a platform, which can provide a

Inktomi's Search Awards

PC Magazine	Editor's Choice Award
PC Computing	Five stars, Excellent
Internet World	Top Search Engine
ComputerLife	Five Stars
Network Computing	Editor's Choice Award

Source: Inktomi Web Page

comprehensive and scalable solution to a host of client needs. Inktomi Traffic Server® is a network cache platform with robust APIs that improves quality of service, optimizes bandwidth usage, and provides a foundation for the delivery of new services at the edge of the network.

For example, Inktomi Traffic Server® Media-IXT™ can easily be integrated with Traffic Server to provide live and on-demand streaming media services. Traffic Server is available in three versions: Traffic Server C-Class for carriers and service providers; Traffic Server E-Class for enterprise networks; and Traffic Server Engine cache appliance solutions, which are available through Inktomi's OEM partners, Intel and 3Com. What makes streaming media (generally video) such a killer application is that it allows a video to be viewed by all users regardless of their connection speeds. Video over the Internet works best with broadband access, of course, but without the streaming media form of presentation it would be nearly impossible for Internet users with 56k access to view the same version of a presentation as those who use DSL, cable modems, or other broadband access. The primary alternative is to produce two (or more) versions, which costs more to create, as well as to store and deliver. Inktomi's Solution Partners have developed extensions on top of the Traffic Server platform, enabling the delivery of services including content filtering to block specific types of undesirable content, authentication, reporting and analysis, and content transformation to enable the delivery of content to wireless devices, such as cell phones.

It is the scalability and the breadth of service that Inktomi offers that should enable the company to build its dominant market position into a very large and profitable franchise over the long-term. A good example of this potential is the recent announcement that Telefonica Data, the data subsidiary of Telefonica group, will be deploying Inktomi's network caching technology across its developing broadband network. This will enable Telefonica to offer streaming media services to its client base. Telefonica's network is expected to eventually offer broadband last-mile access to over half of the Internet users in Spain. The other key element that excites us so much about Inktomi is the corporate culture that has been developed there and the strength of its management team. These factors are critical in fast-growth, high-tech industries where companies live and die based on the quality of their execution.

Company History

Inktomi commenced operations in February 1996, but it really began several years before that on the campus of the University of California at Berkeley. The company's search engine resulted from three years of federally funded research. Eric Brewer, Ph.D. (a computer-science professor at Berkeley) and one of his students, Paul Gauthier, developed a method of harnessing supercomputing power at microcomputer prices. The duo then set about building a team of programmers and began to successfully commercialize the technology. Eric Brewer received his Ph.D. from MIT when he was twenty-five and Paul Gauthier was named the National Science Scholar for the entire country of Canada. According to David Peterschmidt, the current CEO of Inktomi, "they had seven other Ph.D.s hand picked, all under the age of 30, who started the company." (*Greenmagazine*, Ken Kurson, April 2000, p. 2) For Inktomi's fourth fiscal quarter ending September 30, 2000, the company reported revenues of $78.6 million and its third straight quarter of profitability. Inktomi's third quarter revenues grew 27.8% sequentially over the June quarter (or +166.8% per year annualized), which is the kind of financial performance that many companies can only dream of. What is truly special about this performance is the combination of a market dominant position, significant total revenues, impressive growth, and strong profit performance. Solid execution in historical terms doesn't mean the company will perform well going forward, but it's very reassuring to us.

Why is there a Need for Inktomi's Technology?

"More information will be produced in the next three years than has been produced in all time." (*Investor's Business Daily*, Monday, November 6) Chances are that the vast majority of that data will find its way onto the Internet. As Internet usage continues to grow explosively and ever-increasing amounts of data are created, the demand for products that improve the speed and efficiency of the Internet should continue to increase rapidly. Also, it will be critical to have software that effectively categorizes the available information and enables a user to quickly and efficiently sift through the sea of information to find what they really need. "Consider that…all the information in the world today, if stored on floppy diskettes, would create a stack 24 million miles high. The world produced about 1.5 billion gigabytes of information last year. That's 250 megabytes for each man, woman and child, says a study from the University of California at Berkeley. That number—which excludes copies—is likely to double each year." (*Investor's Business Daily*, Monday, November 6, 2000) Luckily, there are some entrepreneurial companies out there which already provide the tools needed to handle this flood of data and Inktomi is the market leader in the area of Internet Infrastructure Software.

Inktomi's products fall into two broad categories: Portal Services (which help the end user find the information or products they need) and Network Products (which increase overall efficiency and optimize the delivery of content and applications for service provider, enterprise and wireless networks).

Portal Services includes Inktomi's search solutions and its commerce and directory engines. Recent estimates place the number of existing web pages at approximately 1.2 billion and counting. (*Investor's Business Daily*, Tuesday, August 8, 2000) Given the size and scope of information on the Internet it is critical that a search engine be well-tailored to its target market. The Inktomi Search Engine is scalable to meet its client's requirements as efficiently as possible. The company's search engine can be tailored to perform regional searches or to provide the robust on-line search support necessary for specialized tasks such as scanning publisher archives. The Inktomi Search Everywhere initiative provides the first fully integrated search infrastructure solution to Internet, corporate and wireless customers, eliminating barriers between previously isolated intranet, extranet, site, and web search applications. The complete offering includes Inktomi Search/Web, Inktomi Search/Custom, Inktomi Search/Site, and Inktomi Search/Enterprise services and products. In keeping with the rapid growth in Internet usage overseas, the company recently announced Inktomi® Search Software 4.0, which enables high quality search performance in most major world languages, including non-Western character sets. Inktomi can also develop private-label web directories based on its Directory Engine. Directories categorize Internet content into areas of interest such as arts, sports, etc. These directories facilitate broader investigation of a topic of general interest.

Rounding out Portal Services is the company's Commerce Engine. The primary factor that draws people to the Internet for retail purchases is convenience. The Inktomi Commerce Engine takes convenience to a whole new level as it facilitates comparison shopping, based not only on price, but by providing useful information so customers can make an informed decision. The Inktomi Commerce Engine provides reviews from *Consumers Digest* and user commentary from *Deja News* and *Delphi*. The Commerce Engine provides scalable, turnkey commerce capabilities for companies in a broad range of markets including portals, destination sites, retailers, banks, credit card services, insurance providers, telecommunications providers, and wireless portals.

Inktomi's Network Products include the Inktomi Traffic Server platform and the Inktomi® Content Delivery Suite. Increasingly rich content such as streaming video can place extreme demand on Internet servers and result in network slowdowns or system crashes. The Traffic Server caching software helps reduce Internet congestion, minimize redundant traffic, and increase network efficiency. Traffic Server stores copies of frequently used information near the user at the edges of the network. Traffic Server can handle over a terabyte of data (or one million megabytes) and is the dominant caching software currently in use on the

Internet. America Online currently uses Traffic Server and is handling approximately seven billion hits per day. Demand for caching products is expanding rapidly, and "revenue in the caching market could total between $6-8 billion by 2004," according to Dane Lewis, an analyst with Robertson Stephens. (Redherring.com, October 23, 2000, p. 2) The Inktomi Content Delivery Suite (CDS) is an integrated solution for content management. "It addresses the fundamental goal of service providers and enterprises: getting the right information to the right person, and at the right time." (Inktomi web site) CDS creates multiple copies of content and synchronizes the delivery of this content to servers across the network. Inktomi's CDS provides a solution that is robust and fault-tolerant. Also, by storing frequently accessed web pages near the user, Inktomi's CDS reduces the time required to download the desired content.

Extending its infrastructure leadership, Inktomi acquired FastForward Networks in September 2000, to create its Media Products Division, developing the first scalable technology for distribution and management of live broadcasting over the Internet.

Competition

Inktomi is active in so many areas that it faces a variety of competitors, but there are no companies exactly like it. In the area of caching software, its primary competitor is CacheFlow, which posted revenues of $22.4 million in its July 2000 quarter. CacheFlow recently announced that it will acquire privately-held Entera to add streaming media and additional content management services to its offerings. CacheFlow offers a caching appliance, which includes hardware as well as software. CacheFlow has been selling its products at a significant discount in order to try and build market share, but it has been losing substantial amounts of money. Inktomi also competes with other companies that offer caching appliances, such as Network Appliance. In the search arena, Inktomi competes with privately held Google, and CMGI-owned AltaVista among others. Inktomi's most important advantages here are that it controls the lion's share of this market and also offers other valuable services, such as its Search Everywhere initiative and Commerce Engine.

Partners and Alliances

As part of Inktomi's ongoing attempt to provide best-of-class service to the end user, the company has joined with other technology leaders to develop the Content Bridge Alliance (see table). Content Bridge is an alliance of leading web-hosting companies, Internet service providers (ISPs), content delivery networks (CDNs) and technology companies that aims to provide the most up-to-date information available as efficiently as possible. The alliance provides a platform for sharing content across networks, which should streamline the link between content providers and end users.

Content Bridge members are able to share information over their networks via Inktomi Traffic Server as the common platform. The alliance is committed to setting open standards, which could include technology from other companies in the future.

America Online will utilize the technology in its network, and Adero will oversee the content management and supply centralized billing services to all Content Bridge members. Joe Barrett, AOL's vice-president for Internet Operations, had this to say about the alliance: "By working with Inktomi and Adero we'll be able to help improve the overall state of

---

Content Bridge Members and Technical Advisory Members

Adero	Inktomi
Digital Island	Madge.web
Sun Microsystems	Compaq
NetRail	Hewlett-Packard
Storage Networks	Mirror Image
Exodus Communications	Alteon
Intel	Vignette
Portal Software	America Online
	Genuity

Source: Inktomi Press Releases

traffic on the Internet by offering both a faster, more efficient experience and an easy-to-use distribution network for all content providers who want to participate." (Inktomi Press Release, August 23, 2000, p. 2) A big part of the alliance's effort centers on developing standards for the distribution and management of content with the goal of improving Internet interoperability. To help further this end, Alteon, Intel, Sun Microsystems, Apogee Networks, Compaq, Hewlett-Packard, Portal Software, StorageNetworks, and Vignette have joined the group as Technical Advisory Members. As stated by Scott Richardson, general manager of Intel's Communications Product Group, "Content distribution and management are vital in enabling the next generation of value added Internet services. We are pleased to be part of the Content Bridge alliance [that is] driving open standards and network interoperability." (Inktomi Press Release, October 12, 2000, p. 2)

The Content Bridge Alliance will compete with Akamai, which operates a proprietary network that is geared to improving the speed and reliability of content delivery. There is also another group called Content Alliance, which was initiated by Cisco and claims Digital Island and Sun Microsystems among its members. There has been an effort by Inktomi to reach out to Cisco and join the two groups into one. (Upside Today, September 25, 2000, p. 2) We believe that it is in everyone's interest to develop one common standard for Internet content management and Internet interoperability. Having a common standard would help improve the reliability and the efficiency of the Internet experience.

Inktomi has also formed several major alliances to help extend its reach overseas. In September 2000, the company announced an alliance with Mitsubishi Electric to distribute Inktomi's Internet Infrastructure software to portals, web-hosting companies and ISPs in Japan. As stated by Koichi Kobayashi, corporate vice-president at Mitsubishi, "Mitsubishi is excited to become an official distributor of Inktomi technology in Japan…We believe Inktomi's cache technology and portal products are key ingredients for the next generation Internet." (Inktomi Press Release, September 20, 2000, p. 1) In Europe, Inktomi has teamed with KPNQwest N.V. and Madge.web. KPNQwest is one of the leading pan-European Internet data communications companies. It is building a 20,000km fiber-optic network—and is one of the largest business ISPs in

Europe, with operations in fifteen countries. KPNQwest will use Inktomi Network Products as "the core enabling technology for efficiently managing, tracking and distributing content and high quality streaming media services." (Inktomi Press Release, July 13, 2000, p. 1) Madge.web operates a global private network, which it calls an Intelligent Overnet that spans fifty-five cities in thirty-three countries. "Inktomi's network cache platform and content distribution technology enables Madge.web to offer global content distribution services designed specifically for content-intensive industries such as financial services and media." (Inktomi Press Release, August 10, 2000, p. 1) Madge.web operates the Madge Broadcast Network, a pan-European, Internet-based broadcast service produced in cooperation with RealNetworks. The company has also announced a global wireless initiative to deliver infrastructure software to wireless network operators, Internet portals, and global enterprises for the delivery of next-generation mobile data services.

Conclusion

Inktomi is uniquely positioned to capitalize on the continuing growth of the Internet. The company is in the enviable position of already being the market leader in software for caching and for Internet search. We believe that Inktomi will be able to leverage this position by continuing to add functionality onto its Traffic Server platform. The company is the nearest thing that there is to a one-stop shop for Internet Infrastructure software.

Inktomi
NASDAQ Symbol: INKT
4100 East 3rd Avenue
Foster City, CA 94404
650-653-2800
CEO David C. Peterschmidt
Web Site www.inktomi.com

Internet Infrastructure Service—Content

InfoSpace, Inc.

InfoSpace

A newlywed couple arrives in Paris and steps off the plane. As they turn their cell phone on, the couple receives a message from their cell phone service provider's "concierge service" that knows their profile (what they like to eat, see, do, etc.). The service knows they enjoy seafood and it suggests the best seafood restaurant in town—with a 20% discount if the couple makes a reservation right then: "Press 1 for a description of the menu and specialties, 2 for directions, and 3 for reservations." The service also suggests several plays that have tickets available, including another discount offer of 20% if booked immediately: "Press 1 for a review of the play and cast, 2 for directions, and 3 for reservations." A few hours before the reservations, the honeymooners are automatically reminded of their reservations along with a map and directions. How did this all happen? The cell-phone carrier uses InfoSpace's service to provide their clients this "concierge service." This is just one way InfoSpace's service can be used to customize mobile service for each user.

Company Description

InfoSpace's software enables the provision of information or the conduction of commerce over any web-ready device, anytime and anywhere. The company provides Internet Infrastructure software to portals (web sites that users tend to visit as an anchor site, like Yahoo!) and other web sites in a private label solution with the customer's name, logo, and color scheme. The result is that InfoSpace is transparent to the end user and is therefore not as well known as some high-profile consumer-related Internet stocks like Amazon or Yahoo.

Company History

InfoSpace is the brainchild of Naveen Jain, whose passion and energy has played a defining role in building the leading wireless Internet infrastructure firm. Naveen Jain emigrated from India in 1979 and later put in seven years at Microsoft, serving as program manager for OS/2 and as a developer for DOS and Windows NT and 95 (for which he holds two patents). He was also the group manager responsible for launching Microsoft's on-line service, MSN. Setting out on his own, Jain used the money earned from Microsoft options to provide the seed capital for InfoSpace, which he started in April 1996. Naveen Jain now serves as chairman and chief strategist for InfoSpace.

Jain sees InfoSpace as providing the tools to build an increasingly diverse, customer-focused web that can function on any web-ready device. The company expects to see Internet traffic shift to smaller, more specialized portals as users seek sites that fit their individual interests—whether sports, women's issues, or teen fare. InfoSpace's Internet strategy is based on the idea that smaller portals will be more likely to continue to rely on the company's services over time, rather than trying to develop an in-house alternative.

In April 2000, Jain brought in Arun Sarin (now CEO of InfoSpace), who had recently served as CEO of U.S. and Asia-Pacific operations for Vodafone AirTouch. Under Sarin's leadership AirTouch grew rapidly from only a single cell-phone license to a global telecommunications company with operations in more than twenty countries. Sarin brings a wealth of contacts in the global telecommunications industry, which should serve InfoSpace well as it attempts to expand its wireless services.

In July 2000, InfoSpace announced the acquisition of Go2Net (which closed in October 2000). This deal dramatically increased both the size of the company and the breadth of its service offerings, including broadband infrastructure services. Go2Net had been developing its business services, such as portal building, which should complement InfoSpace's operations. The company's HyperMart Marketplace features a broad array of services for a base of over one million member businesses. HyperMart offers free web-hosting, turnkey e-commerce and transaction processing services, a "reverse marketplace," business auctions and access to special deals for business shopping. The reverse marketplace allows consumers to detail their needs for everything from web-page design to legal services. Merchants located in the consumer's area can then compete to offer products and services which meet the consumer's needs.

In November 2000, InfoSpace acquired Locus Dialogue, a provider of speech recognition technologies. This move gives the company the ability to speech-enable its existing wireless applications, like its locator services and mobile commerce services. Locus Dialogue's technology had been in development for fourteen years and its products had previously been distributed by major telecommunications providers such as SBC Communications. Locus Dialogue's technology works with a number of different languages, including English, French, and Spanish, and it can simultaneously support bilingual speech recognition.

Primary Product/Service

Technology investors should consider InfoSpace because the company provides an impressive array of services and is well-positioned to benefit from the expected growth of non-PC-based web access. Cell phone use is growing explosively and web-ready phones are catching on. Estimates of the potential market size vary widely, but there could be over 500 million wireless web users worldwide in three or four years. We believe that by the end of 2001, more people will be accessing the web by cell phone and Information Appliances (IA) than by PC. Because InfoSpace currently dominates the wireless web infrastructure market it is well positioned to ride the growth of this trend as it expands from the adventurous early-adopters to a worldwide phenomenon.

Why will so many people want to access the web by cell phones? Web access over the cell phone will bring increased convenience and dramatically enhanced access to information. With the expected increase in bandwidth, a person will be able to do comparison shopping over his phone, easily access maps, or just get directions—and even conduct videoconferences. InfoSpace is already well regarded for its services that use the wireless application protocol (WAP) standard. In February 2000,

Cellmania, a leading provider of mobile-commerce and location-commerce technologies, listed InfoSpace as the best WAP-enabled reference site in the first annual WAPPY awards. WAP provides a text-only version of Internet sites, which can be accessed with tiny cell phone screens. Right now the connection is still slow and functionality is limited. However, with the expected expansion of wireless bandwidth, cell phones will be able to access this information much quicker and will eventually be able to handle graphics as well.

When an Internet user accesses InfoSpace's content, it happens on InfoSpace's servers, unlike with some private-label services. This happens seamlessly so that users get the impression that they are still at the co-branded site. Why is this significant? Advertisers love it. They place one ad with InfoSpace and reach 92% of web users! Because InfoSpace provides services to over 3,100 web sites, it can reach a much broader audience than one portal by itself. Also, the company benefits from its partners' marketing efforts. As they bring in more visitors, InfoSpace makes more money. Over time, InfoSpace has been able to generate a higher level of revenue per pageview. Due to the breadth of its reach, the company even has some content providers paying it to use their material.

InfoSpace lists four of the leading wireless providers in the U.S. among its customers (see table) and claims to reach 80% of U.S. wireless carriers and more than twenty wireless carriers worldwide. The company powers services for over 3,100 web sites, including leading sites such as AOL, MSN and Disney's GO Network. InfoSpace offers an array of information and services including news, search, stock quotes, games, comparison shopping, and more. The company has already begun to span the globe as well. For example, InfoSpace provides infrastructure services to ChinaBig.com, which is the leading supplier of yellow page information to the Chinese community and provides information on millions of companies, products, and services throughout China.

InfoSpace's portfolio of services includes a dynamic pricing service that helps its merchant customers maximize profits by tailoring their pricing based on market demand, inventory level, and customer profile. By using the company's dynamic pricing services, a local merchant can offer discounted prices to customers who live nearby in order to ensure more return visits. That merchant can also offer lower prices to business customers who order large quantities or are frequent customers. Alternatively, a national chain could raise prices on a popular item if demand began to outstrip supply.

Some of InfoSpace's Major Customers

Alltel	Voicestream Wireless	Verizon
ChinaBig.Com	Lycos	Microsoft
SBC Wireless	AT&T Wireless	AOL

Why is there a need for InfoSpace's technology?

There are thousands of web sites on the Internet, and it is much more efficient for them to use a reliable, third-party software provider than to try and reinvent the wheel in-house. By using InfoSpace's technology, a web site can quickly and efficiently offer more services to its customers without the overhead and expense involved in developing it for themselves. Why would a web site provider want to develop their own yellow pages directory when they can just use InfoSpace's tried and true services? Adding more services to a portal or web site means that users stay longer and generate more revenues (from ads or from commerce) for the site.

Also, small businesses will appreciate the HyperMart services which enable them to conduct business quickly and efficiently on-line. The major trend that we believe will drive InfoSpace's growth in the future, though, is the soaring demand for cellular phones and wireless access to the Internet. People have consistently shown that they have an almost unlimited demand for convenience. Why else would everyone own a car? Why else would there by fast food restaurants everywhere and frozen dinners? Wireless access to the Internet means not only increased convenience, but also dramatically increased information that allows people to make better use of their limited time.

Partners and Alliances

InfoSpace makes use of a vast network of affiliates, partners, and alliances that help it leverage its resources to quickly expand its presence over the widest net possible. InfoSpace's goal is to provide relevant, timely information over any web-ready device. To meet this goal, it works with manufacturers like Compaq and Intel to insure that its services will work on any web-ready device. Compaq will use the company's Wireless Internet Platform for its new iPAQ Pocket PC and iPAQ BlackBerry Wireless Email Solution. Together, InfoSpace and Compaq (with its iPAQ offerings) seek to create a comprehensive solution targeted toward the rapidly growing enterprise market. Ted Clark, a vice-president in the Marketing department at Compaq, had this to say about the company's services: "InfoSpace's platform of services is uniquely suited to provide our mobile customers with a powerful wireless Internet experience." InfoSpace private-label Internet services will be available on the new Intel Dot.Station web appliance. Service providers will be able to offer commerce services like locating businesses and comparison shopping based on UPC codes, barcodes, or ISBN numbers. According to Claude Leglise, vice-president of Intel Architecture Group, "InfoSpace's platform offers a fully integrated suite of data transaction services that can be rolled out under any company's brand."

InfoSpace is also working with Nortel Networks in a multi-year strategic alliance to offer the company's wireless services platform in combination with Nortel's network infrastructure products to service providers around the globe. This alliance will seek to enable wireless carriers to roll out advanced data and transactions services quickly over both existing and next-generation (i.e., two-and-a-half Generation and third Generation or Smartphone) wireless Internet networks. Nortel and InfoSpace will also work together to develop new wireless Internet services for 3G networks. The alliance will provide a comprehensive

Wireless Internet platform that is flexible enough to meet its customers' needs and that enables new ways to conduct commerce and communicate. Wireless carriers are making large bets with their investments in next-generation wireless technology. These carriers will need a proven and reliable solution that will help them provide valuable services to the end consumer so as to fully capitalize on their investments.

In another major alliance, InfoSpace and LookSmart agreed to jointly distribute each other's infrastructure services. InfoSpace's infrastructure services platform for branded applications will be distributed to LookSmart's worldwide partners, a network with an unduplicated reach of over 80% of U.S. Internet users. In exchange, LookSmart's search directory will be distributed to InfoSpace's affiliated network of over 3,100 web sites. LookSmart's CEO, Evan Thornley, stated that "By cross-distributing InfoSpace's quality infrastructure services across our network, we're offering small and mid-sized businesses an excellent opportunity to reach a growing on-line audience." The combination means a richer service offering for both companies' customers. In the area of merchant services, InfoSpace partners with a broad distribution network including reseller agreements with regional Bell operating companies like BellSouth and SBC, as well as leading resellers like RH Donnelly and Innuity. The company's merchant services are also available through relationships with merchant banks such as Bank of America and American Express.

Concerns and Competition

One of the primary concerns overhanging the stock in the last half of 2000 has been the Go2Net acquisition. The common wisdom has been that InfoSpace diluted the potential of its wireless operations by acquiring a run of the mill portal. The stock came under heavy selling pressure when the merger was announced and recently sold for $11, down from a high of nearly $140. We believe that Go2Net (which was profitable before the acquisition) brought an attractive portfolio of offerings to the combined company. Go2Net was already developing the HyperMart commerce platform and its web-based payment system. Also, Go2Net was well positioned to offer services in the expanding broadband market that complements the company's wireless strategy nicely. We view the Go2Net acquisition as a long-term positive.

In terms of competition, the combined company faces a variety of competitive pressures on several different fronts. The white and yellow pages information that InfoSpace supplies still accounts for a significant part of its business. The biggest threat here seems to be that the larger portals will try to develop this service in-house. The company has dealt with this by rapidly expanding its client base to over 3,100 web sites, including a host of smaller, more focused portals. These smaller clients will be unlikely to try to develop competing services in-house. In terms of its shopping applications, the company faces competition from Inktomi, among others. Go2Net's Metacrawler search engine competes with Inktomi's private-label search products as well as a variety of smaller competitors. We do not believe that there is any competitive threat that will cause severe harm to the company's business in the near-term. In the wireless infrastructure area (which is probably its most attractive growth prospect), InfoSpace does not appear to have any significant competition. InfoSpace has also taken steps to protect its proprietary technology. The company currently has more than twenty-eight patents pending.

Conclusion

We view InfoSpace as a relatively low-risk way to invest in the coming convergence of wireless and Internet technology. The company is already a dominant player in the fields of Internet Infrastructure and wireless services. Its broad portfolio of service offerings only serves to enhance its attractiveness. We feel InfoSpace will be a leading brand in wireless and Internet infrastructure in this and the next decade.

InfoSpace, Inc.
NASDAQ Symbol: INSP
601 108th Ave NE
Suite 1200
Bellevue, WA 98004
425-201-6100
CEO Arun Sarin
Web Site www.infospace.com

B2B or
Business to Business

Ariba:
Powering the Rise
of the Digital Marketplace

B2B Sector
Description

A purchasing manager for a large architectural consulting firm needs to purchase a new server for her company's growing computer network. She goes on-line to www.Dell.com where she's personally recognized by the site. Here she decides to observe a few educational streaming video presentations covering the latest in new server technology. After the twenty-minute short version of the class, she's ready to place her order. She goes to the purchasing page where she answers a series of questions that help her design the exact system she needs. When she clicks the "order" button, several things happen simultaneously—all of the server parts are ordered from each of the suppliers to be included in the next day's shipment; prices on each of the parts are instantly negotiated via their consortium intermediary site and purchased from the lowest priced, best-of-breed suppliers; time is scheduled the next day on the robotic assembly-line; each specified part is scheduled for receiving and place-ment; and shipping is scheduled for the following day. On the second day, the purchasing manager checks the status of the order on Dell's site where she's able to review each step in the manufacturing process along with the exact time of each step. Within four days, the purchasing manager has her new server.

What is Business to Business (B2B)? It's where one company sells its services or products to another company over the Internet. It's the software platform that allows the above transaction to take place over the Internet.

Most people are familiar with B2C (Business to Consumer) and companies such as Amazon.com and eBay. The transactions in the B2C world usually involve one company and one consumer per transaction, and if something goes wrong, then you have one disappointed consumer. It's completely different in the B2B world. If a transaction fails in the B2B world, it's a different ball game altogether because most of the time there's a contract involved. A delivery failure here might mean not only huge penalties, but also operations shutting down.

The two basic types of B2B models are direct and brokered. The direct model involves one company purchasing from another company directly. The brokered model involves some type of intermediary through which the purchasing company is able to shop around for the best deal. The intermediary might be a person, but it could also be an automated feature in a B2B software package that negotiates for the lowest price amongst several vendors. The most common intermediary is a "vertical portal," where many companies from the same industry come together to set up a virtual buying marketplace for their goods. Here they force the vendors to be competitive with their offerings.

These vertical portals can be small start-ups, groups of companies, or gigantic consortiums created by a particular set of industry leaders. The big consortiums give each member more power to negotiate prices and demand the use of their system.

History—how did it start?

B2B is part of a serendipitous progression of several business productivity trends that have merged together:

- Re-engineering
- Networking of computers
- Internet
- Bandwidth

Each of these trends is part of a larger move toward increasing pro-ductivity and profitability. This trend might not have started with the "re-engineering" era of the last decade, but it certainly did speed things up. The "re-engineering" trend was all about companies becoming more effi-cient and profitable—decreasing expenses. Networking of computers connected us to our co-workers and ended the inefficient sneaker net-work—running floppy disks between each computer. The Internet creat-ed a global network and connected everybody. And bandwidth has enabled us all to exchange huge files of data at light speed.

Security is also a key issue here because we're talking about connect-ing to other companies in a seamless, real-time relationship where confi-dential data can be easily compromised. This is becoming less of an issue with the development of different security technologies such as improved firewalls.

The profitability game is all about increasing revenue and decreasing expenses. Never before have we seen a more powerful tool for business-es to use in winning this game. B2B is so potentially powerful in increas-ing sales and decreasing expenses that it is my firm belief that those com-panies who choose to incorporate B2B technology early-on are most like-ly to dominate their industry or market. Those who wait or don't use B2B at all are just not going to be able to compete—pure and simple.

Future of the sector

Currently, there are several factors limiting this industry at least for another year in the U.S. and abroad:

- Bandwidth
- Complexity, integration, and the time it takes a company to implement B2B
- Old economy businesses not accepting new economy technology
- Employees who fight or are afraid of new technology

Each of these is a short-term problem that will not exist long. The biggest thing holding this industry back is bandwidth, which is fast becoming a non-issue. Currently, with limited bandwidth being such a problem, many clients of the B2B industry are not able to take full advantage of the technology. As the web infrastructure improves with higher bandwidth capabilities, companies will gradually be able to utilize the full capacity of B2B trading schemes. Imagine what real-time two-way video could do for customer support—"Hello, I'm Fred. Can you point your camera toward the damaged equipment so I can take a look at your problem?" As you can see, with bandwidth improvements, these systems will have more potential and more power to transform companies than anything we've seen before.

The design, integration, and implementation process for most B2B customers was difficult at first, but things are changing now. B2B companies are now offering turnkey solutions that are much easier to implement and easier to integrate with administration, manufacturing, inventory, and shipping.

Some companies are just not ready to change the way they do business. This attitude will change gradually as companies realize they must be open-minded to be competitive. This of course gives those who are open-minded already a huge advantage.

These programs must be easy to understand by non-technical people. Otherwise, employees will not easily accept the new way of doing business.

These limitations are much bigger when you step out of the U.S. into other countries where the Internet isn't as developed yet. However, this too will pass as foreign companies begin to face the competition coming from the U.S.

As more people begin to use their cell phones for web access, we will begin to see many Mobile B2B applications being used. Hi-bandwidth, mobile connections will enable the real-time updating of prices and supply information and facilitate the closing of sales. Imagine you are a sales rep on a transcontinental flight and you can collaborate real-time with your customer about an important deal. You could turn wasted time into a videoconference where you both have access to all the specifications needed to close the deal.

Market potential

The industry's implied promise of increased sales and decreased costs for all businesses has created a huge layer of hype. Sources say that the B2B industry in 1999 was approximately $150 billion. The consensus of three-year estimates for B2B range from $500 million to $6 trillion! These figures are for the total volume of transactions which could be conducted on-line. Ariba and other software providers will produce revenues that will be only a portion of this total. However, the companies that do the best job of facilitating B2B transactions will command a highly profitable and rapidly growing business. Based upon my research, most U.S. companies and almost all foreign companies are still not using B2B, especially the smaller and medium-size companies. Knowing that most of them will be using B2B in the future makes this industry THE BIGGEST INVESTMENT OPPORTUNITY I'VE EVER SEEN.

How is this sector changing the world?

First, B2B companies are quickly eliminating the geographic limitations for almost all businesses. Suddenly any business can be global—from Cheeseburger in Paradise in LaHaina, Hawaii, to American Cedar Mill, the cedar-log-home manufacturer in Evening Shade, Arkansas.

Second, the B2B industry is taking a huge chunk out of the threat of inflation. Almost single-handedly, B2B companies are reducing the cost of manufacturing, sales, and delivery. When we order a computer or server from Dell, we use their web site, which automatically designs the computer, creates purchase orders for parts, and manufactures the end product with little if any human contact with the machine. Plus, it's shipped to us within several days of our request. Dell says they do over $42 million per day over their web site! Think about how a manufacturer's bottom line would be improved after incorporating this type of technology in his plant. Think about how much companies could save in payroll expense.

This sector is reinventing the way businesses conduct business. B2B companies offer a combination of two benefits rarely offered and delivered by one company—the potential for dramatically increased sales and decreased overhead. How can they do it? Just imagine Dell computer before the Internet, taking orders and doing business with vendors using paper and fax-based paper ordering systems! I recently stepped into a manufacturing business that didn't even make paper tickets. They didn't have a fax machine and they rarely answered the phone. It was like a Flintstones cartoon.

Technology and the Internet have to a large degree commoditized most industries. At the very least, almost all industries are experiencing more competition than ever before. It's just easier now to do business with any company, no matter where they are located. When an industry is commoditized, the lowest price gets the business. This is frightening for any business owner (and shareholders). This has in turn created several other trends. First, it's forced many businesses to consolidate operations. Second, it's caused many companies to form strategic alliances and partnerships. Never before in the history of the world have we ever seen so many companies initiating strategic alliances and partnerships. The B2B industry makes both of these situations much easier to accomplish.

Structure of this Industry

There are many different sub-groups, but most of them fit into one of these categories:

- e-commerce
- e-purchasing and e-procurement
- e-service
- eLearning and eTraining

We want the Orville Redenbachers (companies that focus on doing one thing well) of the fastest-growing sub-group. The fastest-growing category here seems to be Commerce, and the best B2B e-commerce platform would be the target—something scalable that other companies seamlessly attach themselves to for a synergistic best-of-breed combination of services. Ariba seems to be the best bet.

Ariba:
Powering the Rise of the Digital Marketplace

Ariba provides a software platform that enables corporate buyers and suppliers to interact in a wholly digital marketplace. With features added through Ariba's alliances its customers can handle every aspect of a transaction from gathering information to payment and record keeping within one system. The expected savings from reductions in overhead and economies of scale are tremendous.

Introduction

Ariba offers the broadest e-commerce platform to the widest variety of users on a global basis. The company combines its industry-leading procurement software with a rich array of functions and provides its customers with a completely integrated solution to their e-commerce needs. They don't try to be everything to everyone; they just want to be the best e-commerce platform that's scalable, customizable, and open to other complimentary partners.

Ariba customers can join digital exchanges, which facilitate the rapid exchange of information between suppliers and customers. A company can quickly assess a wide variety of products from competing suppliers to find the one that best suits its needs at the most attractive price. Conversely, suppliers can quickly and efficiently reach a broad spectrum of potential customers with only a minimum of expense. Ariba is playing a key enabling role in fomenting the digital revolution that will transform the global economy.

Company History and Description

Ariba has grown explosively since it was founded in 1996. The company now has 1200 employees and posted revenues of almost $135 million in the three months ended September 30, 2000. Ariba is also nearing profitability as it broke even on an operating basis in the September quarter. Since going public in June 1999, the company has made a few selective acquisitions that have added enhanced functions such as collaborative sourcing technologies that enable buyers and suppliers to locate new trading partners and negotiate on-line. Also, Ariba has been proactive in enlisting partners that could add valuable services for its customers and in setting up alliances with firms such as IBM and i2 to provide a complete solution for developing digital exchanges. Over 100 e-procurement sites and more than 140 digital exchanges run on the Ariba B2B Commerce Platform™. The company's platform includes a comprehensive set of integrated commerce solutions and open network-based commerce services.

The Ariba customer can manage its procurement processes on an enterprise-wide basis, interact with digital exchanges, and sell its goods or services within the same software system.

Why is there a Need for Ariba's Technology?

Ariba's software automates the corporate procurement process and eliminates the need for an army of purchasing agents. The technology goes way beyond simple cost savings, however, in that it enables comparisons between disparate product catalogs from a wide variety of trading partners. Digital exchanges powered by Ariba's Commerce Platform are replacing an older system known as Electronic Data Interchange (EDI). EDI relied on a one-to-one dedicated phone line, which resulted in a costly, cumbersome, and inefficient system. Setting up a dedicated line costs between $25,000 and $40,000, and it still allows communication with only one supplier. The EDI systems weren't economical for handling relationships with smaller suppliers. Now, even small companies can participate in the digital exchange because the cost of connection through the Internet is minimal.

A significant advantage for e-commerce software that is based on the Internet Protocol (IP) is that internal corporate systems will also be compatible with this standard. This compatibility should result in easy integration between external transactions in the digital marketplace and product catalogs, production schedules and other internal systems. The expected savings and improvements from the use of digital exchanges include more effective inventory management, lower transaction costs, shorter purchasing cycles, and lower prices. Collectively these savings should reduce procurement costs by 15-20%. Suppliers should also benefit as the cost of reaching new customers will be greatly reduced and the improved information flow and shorter lead times from e-procurement should also reduce the cyclical nature of many industries. Shorter lead times and better inventory control should reduce the need for companies to overstock, which will reduce the severity of cyclical downturns. These substantial benefits have already caught the attention of most major corporations. According to a survey conducted by Forrester, only 7% of Fortune 1000 firms do not expect to use the Internet for B2B commerce within the next two years, down from 46% in mid 2000. According to

Major Exchanges Already Using the Ariba Platform

Exchange Name	Companies Represented
E2open—global computer, electronics, and telecom	Hitachi, IBM, LG Electronics, Matsushita Electric, Nortel Networks, Seagate Technology, Solectron, Toshiba
Metal Spectrum—specialty metals	Alcoa, Allegheny Technologies, Kaiser Aluminum, Reynolds Aluminum, Thyssen, etc.
Rubber Network	Bridgestone Corp., Goodyear, Groupe Michelin, Pirelli SpA, etc.
Transplace—transportation	Covenant Transport, J.B. Hunt Transport, M.S. Carriers, Swift Transportation, U.S. Xpress Enterprises and Werner Enterprises
Worldwide Retail Exchange	Albertson's, Best Buy, Casino, CVS, Gap, JC Penney, Kmart, Rite Aid, Royal Ahold, Safeway, Target, Walgreens, etc.
MyAircraft/AirNewco—Aerospace	Air France, American Airlines, BFGoodrich, Continental, Delta, Honeywell, United Air Lines, United Technologies, UPS

estimates by International Data Corp. (IDC), a total of $1.8 billion was spent on e-procurement software in 1999. This market is expected to expand at a rate of roughly 67% per year to $23 billion by 2004.

Ariba announced recently (November 30, 2000) their latest version of Ariba Sourcing, featuring an expanded architecture and enhanced navigation and user interface throughout the solution. Additional enhancements include RFQ (Request for Quotation) editing functionality, intuitive graphical user interface with comprehensive field instructions, expanded criteria for supplier capability matching, expanded set of product/service RFQ templates, and expanded registration capability. The new version of Ariba Sourcing is available immediately for buyers and suppliers, but pricing data was not included. This is very important to vendors because Ariba adds important scalability and collaborative and matching functionality that enable the company to target more effectively the direct materials and specifications-based raw-materials market segment. As a net markets infrastructure player, Ariba is the leader and competitors will follow soon to try and match this service.

Why is this market such a big deal? Direct materials or strategic sourcing is a hot topic this year in the e-procurement industry. It's the next phase of e-procurement, which is more complex than the earlier focus, which was primarily on indirect materials that are simpler to transfer to an on-line procurement process.

Digital Exchanges

The race to control the software that powers the new digital exchanges is an extremely high stakes one. There will eventually be only a relatively limited number of exchanges that control the vast majority of B2B e-commerce. The companies using these exchanges will all standardize on the same software platform. About 400 digital exchanges had been announced by May 2000, and some companies estimate that there will be over 11,000 in operation within two years—conducting possibly $1 trillion in annual transactions. Many of the smaller exchanges will probably fold over time as more users migrate to the larger marketplaces in search of a wider customer or supplier base. Ariba already has established relationships with a number of major global exchanges. The alliance between Ariba, i2 and IBM currently powers over 200 exchanges. Some of these exchanges already represent a large number of customers and suppliers. The Worldwide Retail Exchange represents leading retailers worldwide with a total of nearly 50,000 stores and combined sales of over $450 billion, as well as 100,000 suppliers, partners, and distributors.

Customers

Ariba already counts more than twenty of the Fortune 100 among its client list. These critical relationships with major corporations should pay big dividends as smaller suppliers will tend to use the same software as their large corporate customers. This technical lock-in will tend to create a captive audience for Ariba. Also, Ariba is landing deals with major providers of Internet services, which can lead to more converts for the company's software. Digital Insight, the leading provider of out-sourced Internet banking services to more than 880 financial institutions, is using the Ariba B2B Commerce Platform. Lloyds TSB, one of the world's leading banking and financial services organizations, is using Ariba's B2B Commerce platform and has stated that it expects to save approximately $222 million over the next five years through economies of scale and greater supply-chain efficiencies.

Major Ariba Customers

ABN Amro	Digital Insight	American Express
Cargill	Lucent	Honda
Phillips	Visa	Molson
Lloyds TSB	State of California	Sony
U.S. Navy	Bethlehem Steel	Volkswagen

Partners and Alliances

Ariba has a stated strategy that seeks alliances with leading companies that add innovative technology or superior services to complement the company's already strong product mix. Added functionality will play a huge role in the success of digital marketplaces. Previously, procurement officers could bid for products on-line but the rest of the transaction still had to be handled manually. Now Ariba has partnered with several leading finance companies, including American Express, Bank of America, and Visa, to provide integrated financial services along with its B2B Commerce Platform.

Currently, the majority of B2B purchases aren't completed on-line. By integrating services like electronic funds transfers and equipment financing for capital goods, Ariba plans to change that. For more complex purchases Escrow.com will hold the funds until all terms of the contract have been satisfied. In the area of travel services, Ariba has teamed with Sabre to integrate its web-based corporate travel management system. The alliance with IBM and i2 brings a wealth of resources and technical expertise to play in winning contracts with the major digital exchanges. IBM offers its wireless messaging with up-to-the-minute bids that will interact with a wide variety of cell phones and wireless computer devices. Due to its leading position within the procurement software market, Ariba is able to attract service providers with the strongest reputations.

To address the public sector, Ariba has teamed up with Epylon Corp., the leading provider of hosted e-business solutions for education and government institutions. Epylon serves over 1,200 registered school districts and government agencies. Together Ariba and Epylon will develop an integrated platform that is tailored to the needs of public-sector procurement. This service will include Epylon's eQuote and Audit Trail, which satisfy the specialized demands of the public-sector procurement process. The system will also integrate with the existing financial systems already in use by Epylon's customers. Keith Krach, the chairman and CEO of Ariba, believes that the shift to e-commerce in the public sector is still in its infancy.

Ariba is moving quickly to establish a global reach. The company has offices throughout North America, Europe, and Asia. It is establishing an Asian headquarters in Singapore that is well known for its stability and highly skilled workforce. The company expects to help create at least 100 new digital marketplaces in Singapore in the next two years. Ariba has also established several alliances in Asia to better serve the developing markets there. The company has partnered with service providers

Computer & Technology in Hong Kong and New World CyberBase Ltd., in China. Seapower Resources International, the largest cold-storage operator in Southern China, has already created a digital exchange in Hong Kong for the warehousing industry based on Ariba's platform. Ariba has recently taken major steps to expand its presence in Japan as well. The company has partnered with Softbank, which is making a $40 million investment in Nihon Ariba KK, Ariba's Japanese subsidiary, and Softbank will end up with a 40% stake in Nihon Ariba. Softbank is the dominant Internet venture firm in Japan and brings a wealth of contacts and local expertise to bear. We are encouraged by the company's willingness to solicit experienced local partners rather than attempting to go it alone on a global basis.

Competition or Cooperation?

Ariba's single biggest competition is Commerce One, but Ariba came first. Being first should deliver substantial benefits in the digital marketplace arena. The first exchanges to reach critical mass will attract more buyers and suppliers by virtue of their wider reach and lower transaction costs. This dynamic should create substantial barriers to entry and allow the pioneers (namely Ariba and Commerce One) to dominate the software market for digital exchanges. According to Dataquest, Ariba sold 31% of the licenses for e-procurement software in 1999 compared to 20% for Commerce One. They are also the only firms with double-digit market share.

Outside of Commerce One, Ariba has partnered with many potential competitors such as IBM and i2 (the Alliance). This partnership has proven very effective at landing major digital exchanges. However, there is concern by some investors that the Alliance may not be very stable. i2 and Ariba compete with each in a number of ways and there is an outside chance that the Alliance could break down. We view this as unlikely to happen any time soon. The potential benefits to be gained from cooperation are so strong that we believe that the Alliance partners will try very hard to maintain their productive relationship.

The company has also teamed with Bex.com in Singapore, with whom Ariba expects to address the Asian markets. Bex.com is strong in the area of direct materials that are used in constructing a company's primary product. Ariba's software is particularly adept at handling maintenance repair operation (MRO) products that are not resold to customers but used by the company (i.e., office supplies, tools, etc.). Together Ariba and Bex.com can offer "best of breed" services and provide a more complete solution for their clients.

Conclusion

Ariba is addressing markets with enormous long-term potential. The company's dominant position as the market leader in on-line procurement software gives it the opportunity to provide the most comprehensive set of solutions for its customers, which serves to reinforce Ariba's odds for success.

Ariba
NASDAQ Symbol: ARBA
1565 Charleston Road
Mountain View, CA 94043
650-930-6200
CEO Keith Krach
Web Site www.ariba.com

eLearning

Docent Inc.

A services company with 500 employees recognizes the need for ongoing training for employees in the areas of sales, leadership, and specific software packages. After much research, the company realizes the most efficient method of ongoing employee training is custom-designed classes taught by electronic media available on-line. This company forms its own "Corporate University" to meet that need. Fortunately for the company's Human Resources department, this University is up and running within two weeks. Every employee in the company is required to attend the Corporate University and is given access to the classes twenty-four hours a day.

This Corporate University is quite effective in the field, too. One of the company's sales representatives is asked by a prospective client how her company's product solves a specific problem. The rep instantly accesses the company's Corporate University. A brief video demonstration quickly answers the prospect's question. The rep further impresses this prospect by sending him an e-mail with a link to the class to view later. The rep gets the account, and within one week, this new client's entire staff has completed that same course with excellent test scores.

The representative goes home to find that her son has spent the afternoon studying with the world's top high school physics teacher, right in a public school classroom in Middle America, 500 miles away. Her son's class was one of many around the world simultaneously watching this great teacher demonstrate the use of lasers in transmitting huge amounts of data at the speed of light through fiber-optic cable. After this presentation, each student completes an on-line video enhanced test. Their scores are instantly processed. A student may compare his score with a classmate or a student 3,000 miles away by a quick click of the mouse. The representative, her company, and her son have all benefited from this technology. This technology is available for all of us.

Welcome to the world of eLearning. The basic definition of eLearning is the delivery of information (content) by all forms of electronic media—Internet, videotape, CD-Rom, etc. On-line learning can include simple text learning as well as more complex live interactive classroom learning on the web. The term eLearning is also defined as all web and non-web-based electronic training conducted by corporations.

The United States education sector (approx. $750 billion) is the second largest sector of the U.S. economy, second only to healthcare ($1.2 trillion). eLearning is the fastest growing sub-group within the education sector. This is a wide-ranging concept including several different subgroups: K-12, post secondary, continuing education and corporate training. It can also be separated into Business to Consumer learning (B2C) and Business to Business learning (B2B). eLearning's usefulness extends throughout the current (and future) on-line community. Schools use it to teach students around the world. Businesses use it to train staff, conduct meetings, market products, teach customers, certify their partners and suppliers, and share knowledge within the company and across the extended enterprise. This latter view is an educational sub-group of eLearning called B2B eLearning—the fastest growing sub-group within the eLearning category.

Any corporate training done in an electronic format is considered "eLearning." However, for the sake of clarity, I will refer to it as eTraining, even though this term is not used very often in the industry. Training must be a constant, ongoing process for a company to be competitive. The Internet has brought us globalization faster than most people expected, and with this comes intense pressure on corporate executives to expand their enterprises at a very rapid pace. Corporate executives understand that without earnings growth and global expansion, shareholders are quick to put their money elsewhere. The axiom of "sell more and spend less" isn't good enough anymore. Executives know we're in a knowledge economy and that the competition for human knowledge capital is tight and expensive. Companies need a way to develop this human capital inside their own company.

Many very successful corporations today view employee training in a different light than in previous generations. No longer is a one-day seminar, twice a year class sufficient "employee training and development." Each and every task is considered a training session, rather than a one-time goal. Top executives want to create a constant flow of information, theories, questions, innovations (and mistakes) that encourage a team environment of progress and learning within their companies.

The training methods to develop this human capital have evolved from classroom, video, satellite, and CD-Rom to on-line training. Putting together a high-quality, all-inclusive, integrated on-line solution is generally too expensive to do in-house. So corporations must leverage the experience and resources of an eLearning company to custom design their own Corporate University. At its core, a Corporate University must be a comprehensive learning management system (LMS), complete with customized and off-the-shelf courses that can be quickly designed, implemented, and measured for effectiveness. Ideally, all components of a company's value chain—suppliers, production, sales, distribution, and customers—will participate in the company's Corporate University or similar eLearning enterprise.

Studies measuring stock price appreciation have shown that companies that invest in learning outperform companies that don't. eLearning can be a revenue generator helping to facilitate the sale to customers. It builds loyalty with staff and customers as well. An employee or customer who is constantly empowered and challenged with knowledge tends to be more loyal. eLearning has many advantages over traditional classroom learning.

The accompanying table demonstrates the direction of the industry and illustrates attainable goals for eLearning providers within the next two years. While many of the theoretical advantages of eLearning have become reality, quality and content are the two facets of this industry that are lagging behind. Technically, everything exists to deliver the world's greatest teachers and the richest, most engaging content to online students. However, much of eLearning offered today is below this standard. The primary reason is because everyone is in too big of a hurry to focus on quality. There's so much pressure to get the eLearning product up and running that rarely is there time for quality content development. Fortunately, as the best-of-breed education companies come to the web, quality and content will improve dramatically over the next few years.

Advantages of eLearning vs. Classroom learning

	Classroom	eLearning
Access	Structured and limited	24/7 Anywhere, anytime
Pace	Set by instructor	Set by learner—selfpaced
Atmosphere	Foreign place	At home/desk—comfort zone
Quality	Varied	Potential to have the very best teachers
Costs	High	Low
Content	Varied	Potential to have the best content
Results measurement	Difficult	Automatic
Retention of information	Varied	High
Time to learn	Less—forced to hurry	More time to reflect

What's Unique about eLearning?

It can be instantly updated and can always feature the best sources of information. It can be used anytime and anywhere based on the student's own preferences. eLearning's reach extends beyond just "the experts." Students may connect to other students, employees may explore material that exceeds their company's expectations, and experts can talk to other experts. This type of learning experience should be fun, as it often can be customized to the user's favorite format, whether it be text, video, audio, or live classroom. Additional classes can be added easily when requested.

History—how did it start?

eLearning started with computers and video. It gained momentum with the Internet, as web sites began teaching visitors all about their site. The Internet itself is one huge eLearning tool. Today's Internet browser (the first web based eLearning tool) is like a big dictionary, and eLearning solutions are like textbooks.

Today, eLearning has evolved into an interactive medium. Educator and student not only have the ability to communicate from anywhere in the world, but also the ability to simultaneously reference related material. In addition, other on-line visitors can join in the communication live, while each shares a common screen that can be controlled by any one of the participants. This is only the beginning of what is to come in the eLearning industry.

Companies all over the world spend billions of dollars on employee training. With the advent of the Internet and bandwidth improvement, more and more companies want their training available on-line for all their employees. The eLearning industry is growing exponentially to fill this need, but this industry—and eTraining specifically—is still in its infancy.

At first glance, it seems that the comprehensive providers are morphing daily into a "one stop shop." It's their belief that the ultimate goal for most eLearning companies is to be the leading "one stop shop" that empowers client companies or learning institutions to develop their own eLearning sites and programs—very quickly. However, this may not be the best solution. In the long run, eLearning and on-line training can save a great deal of money, because of fewer travel expenses and training personnel needed, for example. This sounds attractive, but it's not easy to set up. Training and architecture must have a user-friendly design. A delivery format must be chosen from the following: text, illustration, video, animation and/or audio. A vendor is needed to provide employees the software (player) needed to view the presentation. Then, everyone has to learn how to use the selected vendor's software. This process is very time-consuming and expensive to implement. The goal of an eLearning solution is to give companies a scalable, turnkey eTraining platform that can be easily customized for the individual needs of the company. The leaders in this industry will be the solution-oriented companies who are fast, independent, and have strategic alliances that give clients access to all available learning tools—not just proprietary ones.

This industry is competitive and growing fast, with over 100 companies fighting for market share, knowing full well that only a good handful will survive in the long run. In 1999 alone, nearly 100 portals were started, and all of them claimed to be the leading eLearning solution. Most of these companies will not be around long. Corporate CKOs and CLOs (Chief Knowledge Officers and Chief Learning Officers) looking for eTraining solutions are frustrated with all the claims. If there are 100 companies all saying they are THE eLearning company, how does anyone make the right decision? Most corporations don't have time to take chances with smaller eLearning firms who offer the one stop shop. They want eTraining partners who will take this burden off their shoulders and add value to their company without taking too much risk. They will recognize quality, leadership, and financial strength and go with the companies that have the best brand names as industry leaders with a proven track record. This is great news for investors because there are only a few solid leaders in this industry.

Future of the sector

The capacity for the individual to educate himself on any topic, anywhere and anytime, is what makes eLearning so attractive. The industry has the promise of explosive results. eLearning providers are now adding many features to their product mix, like:

- Learning management systems—the basic software platform for the whole system
- Authoring tools—software that allows anyone to create a class
- Live collaboration software—such as WebEx
- Knowledge management—keeps track of classes, who's taken what class, performance

- Skills gap analysis—identifies difference between current skills and desired skills
- eLearning consulting—helps client to design, implement, and maintain the system
- Portal customization—clients can custom design their own on-line university
- On-line mentoring—gives class participants the ability to have live tutors 24 hours a day
- Request-for-proposal (RFP) capabilities—clients can custom order a class/system
- Community hosting—ability to host an on-line eLearning solution for any group
- Comprehensive technical support—support that covers everything

Technology must keep up with the growth of eLearning needs. There's a lot of hype about the potential of wireless access to the web. It's estimated that within a year, all-digital cell phones will have WAP (wireless application protocol). It's my firm belief that within one year, we will have more people accessing the web by phone than by PCs. This trend has evolved into "Mobile Commerce" or m-commerce, which gives rise to Mobile Learning or mLearning. mLearning is an exciting sub-group of eLearning. mLearning is where eLearning meets the mobile computer or information appliance (IA). IAs include Smartphones, PDAs, or any other portable hand-held computing device. This amounts to having a supercomputer in the palm of one's hand, with a constant high bandwidth connection to the Internet at all times, anywhere! Just a few of the possibilities this technology can provide to the user anytime, anywhere include: rich, interactive content; fantastic search features; high resolution, full color screen; audio; and performance-based assessment. Input will be keyboard, pen (stylus), or voice activation. mLearning depends upon the IA, which is becoming quite a sought-after item. IAs will become even more commonplace as IA technology improves. Ease of use, cost of operation, bandwidth availability, and features are what make these devices so attractive.

The biggest issue facing the mLearning industry is development. In order to have a successful product, an mLearning company must have quick access to relevant content, get the wireless bandwidth strong enough for IAs, make the unit easy to use and understand, and finally, combine all the technologies together in one package.

All the mLearning companies have their own vision, but these visions don't always blend together very well. Therefore, there's the issue of standards. Most IAs (as well as wireless bandwidth technology) are still in their early-development stages and only offer a limited number of Internet connections. This will not be the case for long. If a specific IA can only get proprietary information issued from limited sources, its customers will not be happy. They will want (and expect) access to all sources of mLearning, in addition to independent access to any available mLearning site.

Market potential

I've seen growth estimates for the eLearning industry that are outrageous. The industry only started a few years ago and is predicted to reach $100 billion by 2003. The sub-group eTraining is predicted by many sources to reach $12 billion by 2003. This is a trend that is not going away. Several sources predict that over 60% of all corporations will have comprehensive eLearning available for their staff by 2003. It's also predicted that a great deal of this eLearning will not only be focused on the employee, but also on the customer and prospective customers. The first wave of growth will certainly be in the corporate arena. The second wave will be in the educational field.

How is this sector changing the world?

Imagine the following scenario: A parent sits in his living room, helping his daughter with her algebra homework by computer. The teenager has at her fingertips access to the key concepts of algebra, broken down into five-to-ten minute learning objects, delivered by the three best algebra teachers in the world, complete with exercises, tutorials, simulations, and every form of learning support imaginable. As this teenager works her way through factoring, a window pops up in the corner of the screen. It's a chat session with all the students around the state who are on-line and have completed this material in the last six months or who are working through it currently. A new window appears visible,only to this particular student, that reads: "Would you like for me to page or call John?" John is the student who, statewide, has shown the greatest aptitude for factoring. The window then reads the following: "I have also noticed that you are doing extremely well in physics. This is an area that John could use some help in. Would you be willing to help John with this?"

After this thorough and effective learning session, the parent goes to bed satisfied that he has really helped his daughter grasp algebra. The lesson, however, doesn't end there. The next morning, sitting in the printer, are five practice exercises to reinforce the concepts studied the night before, a single-page list of the key concepts to remember and a note mentioning that John has accepted the invitation to meet on-line that night for help with his physics.

The eLearning industry will empower the world with learning tools never even dreamed of and will deliver them right to your office, living room, or cell phone. This environment will include story telling, video demonstrations, role-playing, simulations, on-line references, personalized mentoring, discussion groups, tips, tutorials, and wizards. Name the subject and there probably will be an eLearning site ready to teach it. It's just-in-time learning! This will create an education revolution that will make companies more efficient, productive and profitable than ever before. The power of the Internet is not just the content distributed by these eLearning companies. The true power of the Internet is tapped when anyone on the net can author or submit material that can be used to teach others. It's this worldwide, interconnected classroom with many different marketplaces for learning that very few people see and appreciate. Many of the companies only see the corporate training market of eLearning and don't really have a vision beyond that. It's inevitable that the eLearning marketplace will be made up of tens of thousands of learning marketplaces—companies, K-12, colleges, continuing education, churches and organizations. The winners in this industry are the ones who share this vision.

The World of eLearning

Within the corporate training market (approximately $63 billion), only a small fraction is web-based or technology based, but this is growing rapidly. There are many eLearning companies competing for market share. Many are trying to put together the one stop shop, while others are focusing on one single area. Picking the right company to hire as your eLearning solution (much less a company to invest in) is tough, unless you understand the structure of the industry. There are three sub-groups:

eLearning Sub-groups

LMS/Technology—software, Learning Management System (LMS)

Content—providing a course catalog to choose from

Services—consulting, measurement, authoring tools, custom content design

The basic infrastructure of any comprehensive eLearning solution is a combination of these three pieces: Learning Management System (LMS), content and services. The LMS is the software or platform within which all of the learning takes place. It's the engine that runs the entire system, or if one prefers, the platform upon which everything else is placed. Content includes all of the classes and applications that are geared toward teaching the students. Services host a myriad of applications: assessment of needs, testing, measurement, integration services and performance measurement.

To truly explode as an industry, there is a fourth piece that a few eLearning companies must recognize: marketing. This can include aggregation as well as more traditional marketing. Marketing is important to companies promoting eLearning providers, but also in interconnecting to them. That's where the true power of the web comes in.

This industry is growing so fast that, in our opinion, it will look totally different in eighteen months. The speed of growth in the industry and the number of companies claiming superiority can make a company's eLearning decision difficult.

The eLearning Solution

Below is a list of features that most corporations are looking for in a total eLearning package. Some companies try to offer all of these features, while others focus on just a few.

- Brand name—a company with experience and national presence
- Assessment analysis—what does this include or involve?
- Curriculum design and development
- Authoring tools
- Easy access to classes
- Large catalog of proprietary and non-proprietary classes
- Custom classes available
- Personalized service for each learner, including on-line mentoring
- Access to fellow learners (live and message)
- Tools for evaluating progress of each individual and the whole system
- Integrated and scalable—easy for any size company to use
- Comprehensive Learning Management System—the whole package and system hosting
- Live on-line classes with recording capability ("surrounds")
- Web-based training that is accessible anytime and anywhere
- mLearning capabilities

Conclusion—Best-of-breed integration

Many companies will fall for the beauty of an eLearning one stop shop. The term "one stop shop" in the eLearning industry commonly refers to companies that are trying to provide an LMS, all the content, and all the services together. While this may seem like the Holy Grail of the eLearning industry, it actually is somewhat of a trap. Anyone looking for an eLearning solution (CLOs, schools, organizations) must have access to the very best pieces of the eLearning solution. One firm can't have all the best pieces in-house. How can any company have all the best-of-breed players in-house at any one time? The solution is going to be a combination of the best practices partnered with preeminent providers all working together for the client. The future leaders will be the ones who can foster an environment where specialists can partner freely. The only sub-group that can really offer this is the LMS/technology sub-group mentioned earlier in the chapter. This is the neutral ground or software platform upon which service and content providers can build their partnership foundations.

There's a lot of competition in this field. The best investment in this sector is going to be the company that has the least competition in combination with the strongest business model within the industry. The most competitive sub-group seems to be in the content-provider sector where there are so many companies. The least competitive sub-group seems to be the companies that focus primarily on the LMS/Technology or software platform upon which everything is based. What Intel is to the computer industry, platform is to the eLearning industry. My theory is: why invest in the end product companies when one can own the chip in every one of them—"the Intel inside?" The only company I could find that focuses 100% on the platform is Docent. Saba Software would be a close second choice.

Obstacles in the Expansion of eLearning

The primary obstacles in the expansion of eLearning include: bandwidth limitations (slow Internet connection), limited content (few classes available), absence of common standards (we must have common software standards so anyone can access the classes from their computer), and segmented features/services (we need a comprehensive solution that is integrated together seamlessly). Fortunately, these obstacles are being overcome quickly by the industry.

Other major obstacles include the one stop shop concept and general ignorance and confusion surrounding the industry. It is impossible to be a one stop shop with everything in-house and expect to be the best in all the service and product categories! We firmly believe that eLearning companies must decide upon their key competencies and focus their efforts on being the best at one thing and then partner with other companies to provide all the other pieces. The final obstacle is the confusion that surrounds all the eLearning solution options. It's difficult to identify what is currently available and even harder to predict what the industry will look like in the very near future. We believe that it would be a mistake to simply ignore this industry or shy away from investing in it simply because of a lack of knowledge or familiarity.

The eLearning Stock that Could Change the World—Docent, Inc.
Company Description

Docent Inc. (DCNT), based in Mountain View, California, has the potential to be the eLearning platform of the future. The company intends to be the very best eLearning platform. Docent's core competency is LMS. They partner with the best providers for content and services, offering their clients a superior customized solution.

Company History

In January 1991, Pardner Wynn founded Stanford Testing Systems, a provider of test-preparation and skill-assessment software. The company went to the web in 1995 with its free SAT test preparation product. The system scored students' results and helped them identify exactly what areas needed improvement. It also gave Stanford Testing a great database of students that soon evolved into an important revenue generator for the company. Later that year, parents of the students began asking for similar testing for their companies. Many of these parents were executives at large companies such as Boeing, IBM, and Tektronix. After about fifteen calls, Mr. Wynn decided he might have the ingredients for a new company. In October of 1996, David Mandelkern was hired by Wynn at Stanford Testing Systems as a consultant. Mr. Mandelkern founded and served from July 1993 to June 1997 as President of AlmondSeed Software, a provider of UNIX utility software. Together Mr. Mandelkern and Mr. Wynn started Docent in June of 1997.

In July of 1998, they hired Dave Ellett as Chief Executive Officer and President. After serving on the board since March 1998, Ellett was elected Chairman of the Board in January 2000. Dave Ellett has a proven track record. From April 1997 to July 1998, he served as Chief Operating Officer of Business Objects, Inc. (BOBJ). During his term, BOBJ's stock more than doubled, beating the NASDAQ by a substantial margin. Since then, the stock is up almost 1,000%. From January 1994 to April 1997, Ellett served as Corporate Vice President of Worldwide Education at Oracle Corporation. In addition, Ellett spent thirteen years at Electronic Data Systems, most recently as President of the Performance Services

Group from 1991 to 1994. He holds a B.A. degree from Southern Methodist University.

Dave Ellett's personal and corporate mission to change the world of education is a huge selling point for the company. When I recently interviewed him for this book he said, "What you are writing about is why I came here—to change the world. It's not about money. It's about making a real difference and that's what we're doing." Ellett's vision is to provide a platform that can work for anyone—from K-12 to corporations. He wants to make eLearning available and easy for five year olds as well as senior citizens. He told me, "We want to produce a platform that allows the user to also be a creator, so that anyone can put their message out there. Imagine every high school in the world able to connect with the best high school physics teacher in the world! eLearning can capture the teacher's best work live, replay a recording later and enable students to share their observations with the instructor and other students from anywhere in the world." Ellett added, "If you take away the gating item out of the educational process, you make the content easy to publish and make it available to everyone."

Docent's Primary Product

Docent has one product—Docent™ Enterprise. This is an Internet-based software platform for knowledge exchange that goes beyond the delivery of learning content on-line, commonly known as eLearning, to bring together organizations into a virtual marketplace with an array of value-added features. Docent provides a platform that can be used by many different customers such as corporations, content providers and professional communities.

- *Enterprises* or large organizations can create, deliver, and manage educational content targeted to the needs of employees, customers, and partners, providing a measurable impact on business performance.
- *Content providers* or companies that develop educational material can generate additional revenue by bringing their offerings on-line and participating in virtual knowledge marketplaces.
- *Professional communities*—such as stockbrokers, managers, and

consultants communicating through the Internet—can offer a broad range of educational content from multiple sources as well as skill assessment and performance tracking.

Docent understands the needs of the industry's clients. They want to provide clients with learning tools that are completely integrated in the daily tasks of their work. The following is an example what such systems can do: At an investment advisory firm with full eLearning capabilities, if an advisor makes a mistake in setting up a stock transaction for one of his clients, the system will recognize that mistake and provide a guide demonstrating proper procedure. In addition to the tutorial, by audio track or simulation, the system lists other clients that may benefit from that same transaction. The system also explains how it calculated its list and why. In addition, the system queues up and automatically schedules a fifteen-minute learning object on portfolio strategies from the New York Institute of Finance for the advisor. The system may then run the advisor through a quick assessment of the advisor's comfort level in making the transaction for his clients. Based on this assessment, it proposes developmental interventions to address the advisor's weakness. To motivate the advisor, the system presents the average difference in annual rates of return and risk factors for each portfolio, given the growth estimates for each stock transaction. It also shows how this skill correlates to the advisor's indicated long-term career track towards an executive office in the firm.

Competitors

This sector is growing fast enough to support many different companies. After talking with several CEOs within the eLearning industry, I'm convinced that currently there's very little actual head-to-head competition, because most of the leading companies are scrambling just to fill all the orders coming in. However, this will not last forever. Each will evolve into what they think is the right business model. Until then, a lot of changes will be seen within these companies. Some of these companies are both competitor and partner. For example, SmartForce has content that Docent has access to as a partner, but they both have a competing LMS/platform technology. It can certainly be confusing.

Below we've organized the companies within the different categories, starting with Docent's leading LMS platforms competition.

Saba Software Inc. (SABA)
www.saba.com
2400 Bridge Parkway
Redwood Shores, CA 94065
650-696-3840
CEO Bobby Yazdani

Docent's primary competition is Saba, which also wants to be the platform of choice for the eLearning industry. They are a strong competitor with more than 3.2 million users, over 30,000 classes and over three times more revenue than Docent. Saba went public before Docent in early April of 2000. Their company's Saba Learning Enterprise system won a Crossroads 2000 A-List Award in the Strategic Software Platforms category as the best, newly proven technology for "Technology Infrastructure." The decision between Docent and Saba was tough, as both are excellent companies. However, Docent has three advantages over Saba.

First, the CEO of Docent, David Ellett, has an extraordinary desire to "change the world." I am impressed by his dedication to eLearning and his drive to make Docent a role model and leader in this industry. Second, Saba isn't a true "Orville Redenbacher." Instead of trying to be the best at one thing, they have several product groups and have strayed away from being a platform-only company. Therefore, it's my belief that Docent's single-minded focus on a highly competitive platform is a strategic advantage over Saba. Third, Saba is based upon a client-server system, which requires the user to have Saba software. Docent is born on the web and is much more flexible to use and manipulate.

Learning Management System Competitors

Below are companies with proprietary Learning Management Systems (LMS) platforms that compete with Docent. Most of these companies have extensive content partners.

- Saba (see above)
- Click2Learn (CLKS), www.click2learn.com, Bellevue, WA
- Lotus Development Corp., www.lotus.com, Cambridge, MA, subsidiary of IBM
- WBT Systems (private), www.wbtsystems.com, Waltham, MA
- LearnFrame (private), www.learnframe.com, Draper, UT
- Teamscape (private), www.teamscape.com, Burlingame, CA
- Berkeley International Capital Corp.

One Stop Shop Competitors

The companies listed below seem to be focusing on being the one stop shop solution for eLearning. Some are competitors and some are partners.

- DigitalThink (DTHK), www.digitalthink.com, San Francisco
- Smartforce (SMTF), www.smartforce.com, Redwood City, CA
- Learn2.com (LTWO), www.learn2.com, White Plains, NY
- KnowledgePlanet.com (private), www.knowledgeplanet.com, Reston, VA
- THINQ/Training Server (private), www.thinq.com, Billerica, MA, merged 10/25/00
- Headlight.com (private), www.headlight.com, San Francisco, CA
- EMind (private), www.emind.com, Los Angeles, CA
- Mentergy (private), www.mentergy.com, merger of Gilat, Allen, & LearnLinc

Content Providers

The companies below are all on-line learning and training companies that publish and offer eLearning and eLearning classes.

- Smartforce (SMTF), www.smartforce.com, Redwood City, CA
- Ninth House Network (private), www.ninthhouse.com, San Francisco
- Teach.com (private), www.teach.com, Elk Grove, IL
- DigitalThink (DTHK), www.digitalthink.com, San Francisco
- NETg, Subsidiary of Harcourt (H), www.netg.com, Naperville, IL

- Cognitive Arts (private), www.cognitivearts.com, New York
- SMGnet (private), www.smgnet.com, Philadelphia, PA
- SkillSoft (SKIL), www.skillsoft.com, Nashua, NH
- KnowledgeNet (private), www.knowledgenet.com, Scottsdale, AZ
- MindLeaders.com, www.mindleaders.com, Columbus, OH
- Quisic (private), www.quisic.com, Los Angeles
- Devry (DV), www.devry.com, Oakbrook Terrace, IL
- Provant (POVT), www.provant.com, Boston, MA
- New Horizons Worldwide (private), www.newhorizonsworld-wide.com, Seattle, WA
- Learning Tree International (LTRE), www.learningtree.com, Reston, VA
- ARIS Corporation (ARSC), www.aris.com, Bellevue, WA
- Franklin Covey (FC), www.franklincovey.com, Salt Lake City, UT
- Global Knowledge Network (private), www.global-knowledge.com, Atlanta, GA
- ExecuTrain (private), www.executrain.com, Atlanta, GA

These companies also provide on-line classes, but they are licensing agents that offer classes from various sources:

- Pensare (private), www.pensare.com, Sunnyvale, CA
- UNext.com or Cardean University (private), www.unext.com, Deerfield, IL

What Makes Docent Unique?

Docent is different from the rest of the eLearning pack in several ways. First, the company's vision is a knowledge exchange, where there are many knowledge marketplaces each connecting thousands of providers. Docent has a firm grasp on "the big picture" of the industry's potential and how Docent can contribute to making that potential a reality. They want to be the platform of choice in the eLearning industry.

Second, they follow Orville Redenbacher's motto: "Do one thing and do it better than anybody." They feel that trying to be a one stop shop would be a mistake, detracting from the company's greatest strength. They feel the better strategy is to focus on being the best platform for any eLearning application and then build strong alliances or partnerships with other companies to provide all the other pieces. This gives each client the ability to design his own program of best providers. Their web site sums it up this way: "Docent's strategy is to become the platform for the broadest range of eLearning solutions on the market. To achieve this objective, we focus our development efforts solely on the Docent Learning Management System—not content or authoring tools or anything else."

Third, Docent is a Learning Management System (LMS) and a Content Delivery System (CDS), which is a unique combination in the industry. They can manage all the intricacies of the learning module, deliver and manage any kind of content, and collect every click for archives and comparisons. SABA does not have a CDS managing the content. Therefore, users are unable to have much flexibility with their content, specifically in scoring results and overall performance assessment.

Fourth, Docent is well ahead in the mLearning trend. Their LMS/platform is a true mobile and wireless product that can be downloaded or accessed by a PDA or cell phone. Their pure web architecture gives them much more flexibility.

Fifth, they are strategically focused on partnerships in all the other areas so that any organization or learning marketplace can use their platform and design exactly what they want. Docent does not want to be in any other business.

Partnerships and alliances

Partnerships and alliances are certainly nothing new in this industry, but Docent makes it one of their top priorities. Because Docent is only an LMS/platform, they depend a great deal on alliances and partnerships with other firms for content and services. Dave Ellett says that one of the company's top priorities is securing partnerships with best-of-breed providers. Docent has an extensive partnership list and divides their partnerships into unique categories.

- Sales Partners sell and/or integrate eLearning solutions to specific markets in on-line communities and may resell the Docent/Partner solution in conjunction with their value-added services. This category includes companies such as Anderson Consulting, Deloitte Consulting, Hewlett-Packard Education, and the Global Knowledge Network.
- Content Providers provide course content or competency models and partner with Docent to develop an eLearning business. SmartForce, TRG, Harvard Business School Publishing, and FT Knowledge are a few of the companies in this category.
- Enterprise Consumers are Fortune 2000 enterprises and others that use Docent products to educate their employees, customers and partners. They also purchase Docent software and services directly to create eLearning systems for their organization or customers. The list includes Pitney Bowes, Schering-Plough, and TIAA-CREF.
- Destination Communities and/or web affiliates provide Internet portals that distribute education content to their members. The National Association of Manufacturers Virtual University and Portera are just two examples.
- Implementation Partners repurpose course content for the web, customize Docent for integration with enterprise systems, and/or provide hosting services. Anderson Consulting, Deloitte Consulting, Quisic, C3i, Learning Voyage, and Rapid Learning Development are included here.
- Complementary Partners co-market their solution with Docent to specific markets. This includes synchronous vendors who do not resell Docent, complementary technology vendors with potential to integrate or bundle with Docent, and complementary technology that runs on Docent. Members include Centra, InterWise, Microsoft, Oracle, PlaceWare, WebEx, and Siebel.

Conclusion

There are many fantastic companies in the eLearning industry, and for now it might be easy to make a profitable investment. However, as more private companies go public and the competition intensifies, only a few eLearning companies will do well. The investor needs to look for the company that is going to not only survive, but also thrive in the long term. It is my belief that Docent fits these criteria, in spite of its small size relative to the other leaders in the industry. It has tremendous growth potential and an opportunity to be the best in the eLearning software-platform sector.

Docent Inc.
NASDAQ Symbol: DCNT
2444 Charleston Road
Mountain View, CA 94043
650-934-9500
888-DOCENT-5
CEO Dave Ellett
Web Site www.docent.com

Web-Conferencing

WebEx

Web-Conferencing Sector
Leading Story

A top management executive, after reading a white paper on her company's industry, finds a software company that has the potential to revolutionize her company and make the business 50% more efficient. She reads about this software company's service, technology, and success on their web site. After contacting the company, the executive asks them to visit her company's facility to demonstrate the software and its capabilities to her management team. Instead of booking a plane ticket, the software company's representative says, "Let's set up a web-conference call." The executive thinks this is "just a conference call" and would rather have an expert over her shoulder explaining the software. The software company rep explains the concept and says, "We'll demonstrate the software and let you take a test run using the web and phone."

Two days later, the management executive and her team (from several locations around the world) are all on a conference call by phone and simultaneously on the web, listening and watching their screens while the representative demonstrates the software for everyone. The software company rep then allows the executive to control the demonstration by switching control from his machine to hers with just a click of the mouse. The management team observes it all as they listen by phone and watch every move their boss makes on their screen. After agreeing to try the software for a week, the management team is led through a live training class by the software company. Welcome to the world of web-conferencing. This is not the future—it's now!

Web-conferencing

The name "web-conferencing" alone doesn't do this sector enough justice. A better name for this sector would be "live interactive multimedia communications." Techies refer to this sector as "synchronous web communications." For now, let's just call it web-conferencing.

What is web-conferencing? It's live (real-time) discussions over the Internet using visually oriented material such as software applications, documents or anything that can be seen on a computer screen. In other words, it's an on-line meeting where you can share anything you want from each other's computers.

This sector is unique because it's a crossover sector—a sub-group of several different larger sectors. Both of the larger B2B and eLearning sectors utilize this technology.

History—how did it start?

The web-conferencing industry evolved as busy business people became more demanding of their communication tools. E-mail and attachments can go only so far in terms of communication. Nothing can take the place of live, interactive meetings or discussions where two or more parties can exchange visual content, whether that be software, documents, or family photos. Many people believed that simple videoconferencing—live video via phone or satellite—would be the answer, but it falls short of most expectations, because there's no way to interact. It is not just the sharing that's important. What is needed is a way for a team of people, scattered all over the world, to work on and complete a project by discussing, researching, writing, editing, and exploring scenarios *together*.

What else is driving this industry trend? Traveling has become not only expensive, but it can be extremely time-consuming. The Internet is changing everything, including live meetings. Web-conferencing is the bane of most travel agencies. I spoke with a software company rep in Memphis who started using web-conferencing to sell his product. He said his travel expenses went from $80,000 to $2,000 in the first year.

The eLearning trend alone is big enough to drive this industry. The globalization of the corporate world is causing companies all over the world to train their entire staff with new technologies and procedures. Getting every associate together in one place is almost impossible, if not completely cost-prohibitive. Web-conferencing is the answer.

With increased competition and pressure from stock markets to perform well and fast, there's an ever-increasing need for companies to get new products to the marketplace quickly. Web-conferencing is the competitive advantage that makes this possible.

Today's integrated businesses must be able to communicate well not only with staff, but also with clients, partners, and even suppliers. Web-conferencing empowers everyone.

Future of the sector

The leaders in this industry will say they are on the cutting edge of the "Real-time Revolution." This revolution is all about conducting meetings in real time, one-on-one or with several participants, on the Internet without having to travel anywhere. This is more powerful than teleconferencing. This technology gives its users the advantage of sharing products, presentations, and ideas with anyone, anywhere, anytime without leaving their computer screens. Co-workers can call each other and surf the web in tandem to find a solution to a client's problem and then demonstrate the solution to the client. Those co-workers can then call their out-of-town colleague, take control of his computer software, and walk him through their solution.

Users can benefit from the "real-time revolution" in their personal lives as well. For example, a grandchild can call her grandmother and record a special holiday recipe on the family homepage, including digital photos of them making it together. These are just a few of the possible scenarios. This technology is here today—it is just not owned by many people yet. It will be very soon.

Market potential

The market is huge and growing fast. *Everyone* can use this technology. Corporations, organizations, schools, and even families all have a need for this technology. Currently, the primary market is corporate, but its uses within that market are diverse. First, it's being used to conduct live intra-company meetings. Second, it's being used for learning and training. Third, it's being used to market and provide service to clients. Fourth, it's being used to communicate with vendors. Soon this technology will be used by individuals outside of the corporate world.

How is this sector changing the world?

What percentage of the economy depends upon the human interaction of at least two people in a meeting that results in a transaction? Most esti-mates I've seen are around 50%, but I'm convinced it's even higher, espe-cially in the service business. The effectiveness of this human interaction is directly related to the quality of communication, which can certainly be enhanced given current technology and the overwhelming amount of data that's available today on any given subject. The key to successful com-munication today is the ability to make it simple and convenient to get your point across to others.

Having said that, think about the potential of having at one's finger-tips a communication medium that combines the power of audio, visual information, data, video, and the Internet. A person could be anywhere in the world and participate in any meeting or class, in real time and inter-actively. Now imagine even further that this medium becomes as much a common practice as using the telephone! Now that is a whole different world. That world exists, it is just not widely known yet. The ultimate goal of the leaders in this industry is the development of the real-time web.

The Web-Conferencing Company that Could Change the World—WebEx: Company Description

WebEx is the leader in the real-time virtual-meeting market. They provide interactive multimedia communication services that enable any-one with a web site to become meeting enabled. They provide a network, as well as a scalable platform (meeting portal) that can be leveraged by their partners in providing customers reliable, secure meetings on the web.

Company History

The company was started by Subrah S. Iyar and Min Zhu, who are now the CEO and Chief Technical Officer respectively. Subrah's background includes fifteen years of sales and marketing. He was instrumental in creating the first Operating System licensing business in Apple's Newton Group. At Intel he held several positions in product marketing and OEM (Original Equipment Manufacturing) sales management within the LAN software and systems group. Subrah was also vice-president of sales, marketing and business development at Teleos Research, which was acquired by Autodesk. In 1995, Subrah joined Quarterdeck Inc. as vice-president and general manager of the company's Northern California Internet business division. He was also president of Future Labs, a Quarterdeck subsidiary. Subrah holds a B.S. in Electrical Engineering and an M.S. in Computer Engineering.

Min is the genius in the back. His career spans fourteen years, including experience with mainframes, database systems, networking and communications, telephony, PC collaboration software and expert systems. Min developed his technology expertise at the IBM Scientific Center in Palo Alto. He was also the deputy to the chief technical officer of Price Waterhouse and the vice-president of Expert Edge, a software design company. In 1991, Min co-founded Future Labs (one of the first companies to produce multi-point document collaboration software). Quarterdeck acquired Future Labs in 1996, and Min went on to co-found WebEx. Min holds an M.S. in Engineering from Stanford University.

Min's success today is a reflection of his courage and tenacity, which is even more amazing when you know where he began his career. Min was born and raised in China. At the age of seventeen, he had just completed high school and was an excellent mathematician. The Cultural Revolution changed everything for him. He was sent to what he calls "the countryside" where he spent eight long years as a farm laborer. Today, he's the Chief Technology Officer of a company that could change the world. His life is truly a rags-to-riches story.

Min and Subrah met when Min's company Future Labs was acquired by Quarterdeck, where Subrah was working as the VP.

Description of product/service

WebEx offers any company or individual the ability to conduct real-time meetings over the web between two or hundreds of people. Each participant dials into the meeting either via conference call or direct. Simultaneously, they go to a designated web site and click a button to join the meeting. Once there, they can participate in the conference call as their screen becomes the meeting leader's screen. Whatever the meeting leader does on his or her screen is seen by the participants. This alone is a fantastic product, but there are many other additional features that make it even better.

What is more important is that this same service is also offered as a platform or infrastructure for other web sites, such as Yahoo! and Global Crossing, to enable their customers to conduct real-time meetings. For example, WebEx signed an agreement with Yahoo! Inc. (NASDAQ: YHOO) to become the premier web-conferencing solution provider for Corporate Yahoo!™ (http://corporate.yahoo.com), a customized enterprise information portal based on the widely used My Yahoo! (http://my.yahoo.com) interface. Corporate Yahoo will in turn promote and position these interactive services to customers as a way for them to conduct real-time multimedia meetings on their web sites to enhance business communications in areas such as sales, marketing, training, support, and partner management.

WebEx has three tiers of communications infrastructure. The first is their Interactive Services tier, which is the real-time interactive meeting service for both businesses and individuals. The second tier is the Interactive Platform, which is offered to other partners such as Yahoo and Global Crossing. The third tier is their Interactive Network of servers that support the volume of business.

- Interactive Services (businesses and individuals)
- Meeting Center
- Business Exchange
- On-Call
- Interactive Platforms (partners)
- Meeting Manager
- Session Manager

- Telephony Manager
- Office Manager
- Interactive Network
- 120 servers and six hubs in U.S., Europe & Asia

Let's take a look at each of these areas in more detail.

Interactive Services
WebEx Meeting Center

The Meeting Center is where it all begins. Each participant has the ability to use any of the following features as he participates in the meeting:

- Presentation sharing—this allows anyone in the meeting to share any presentation at anytime without having to upload the file where the security of the file could be compromised. Participants could even be taken on a web tour. Anything that is on the main presenter's screen will be synchronized in "real time" on the participant's screen.
- Document sharing—this allows anyone in the meeting to view any document or graphic with high resolution, zooming capabilities, and annotation. The annotated document can be saved for later viewing.
- Application sharing—allows participants in the meeting to run any software application for effective live demos and training. The presenter shares control of any software application with participants.
- Web co-browsing—enables two or more people to browse the web.
- Remote control—enables one to (with permission) take control of another's computer and vice versa. This is great for computer software support.
- Polling—this lets presenters solicit feedback from attendees on-line.
- Desktop Sharing—this feature allows participants to share control of any of the participants' PCs (with user's approval) to instantly

access an application—edit, cut and paste, draw, annotate, high-light, etc.

- Scalable—allows there to be as many participants as needed in a meeting.
- Internet voice—allows the use of IP telephony instead of regu-lar phone lines if desired.
- Security—allows one to offer unlisted meetings, password pro-tected and encryption to protect confidential data.
- Video Integration—video conferencing is easily enabled with a simple desktop video camera. Participants can see live video even if they are behind a firewall.

WebEx Business Exchange

This is a personalized virtual office space for your company where WebEx has bundled several different services into one platform. This ser-vice can dramatically improve the efficiency and speed of execution of meetings in any business that requires meetings.

There are six parts: Meetings, Office, Business Directory, OnCall, OnStage, and MeetingAssist. The meeting center feature is the same as mentioned above.

WebEx Office is a virtual office space on the web where staff can instantly initiate an on-line meeting with anyone inside or outside the company. From this office web site, employees or customers can access and even download shared information such as files, presentations, or even recorded meetings. Visitors can submit requests for meetings and even access the meeting schedule. This also includes messaging, public and private folders, and web pages.

WebEx Business Directory gives visitors to your site's home page an easy way to locate your virtual office on the web. They can search by name or even multiple categories to make it easier to locate you on-line.

WebEx OnCall is the future of customer support. It allows company representatives to instantly initiate live on-line sessions so they can diag-nose and fix problems using powerful interactive tools. This includes installation and configuration of any software. Using WebEx's remote con-trol feature, the representative can take full control of a customer's com-puter system if the customer desires. This service can also help facilitate the downloading of software updates and files at anytime.

WebEx OnStage is a fully integrated on-line seminar hosting service that can assist in everything from expert planning advice to execution and real-time support. This service is for larger meetings.

WebEx MeetingAssist is a support service for smaller on-line meetings, which includes planning, rehearsals/walk-throughs, slide optimization, and technical assistance.

It's important to remember that everything above can also be used by individuals. There is a personalized virtual-office service designed especially for individuals. It consists of Meetings and Offices. The Meetings feature is again the same as above. The WebEx Offices for individuals is very similar to Offices for businesses.

Interactive Platforms

This service offers companies an opportunity to sell or provide these same meeting services to their customers. There are three types of partner relationships. First is WebEx for resellers, which allows other companies to resell WebEx's services. Resell partners include Tibco, SmartForce, and Yahoo. Second is WebEx for telecommunication providers, which gives telecommunication vendors a conferencing solution for their existing clients. Partners include Global Crossing, MindSpring, and Deutsche Telekom. Third is for Business Portals & On-line Service Providers who want to add free and pay-per-use WebEx services to their web sites. Partners include Buzzsaw.com, Sales.com, and Adobe.

- Session Manager verifies the authenticity of each participant, sets up new meeting sessions and terminates sessions at the end of each meeting.
- Meeting Manager provides the core real-time data conferencing capabilities.
- Office Manager provides the tools that organize the WebEx meeting. This feature enables users to set up individual outer offices for sharing content information, schedules, and files with others who visit the company or portal Business Exchange.
- Telephony Manager integrates voice communication for the meeting.

This tier of service is one of the most important aspects of this company. It's one thing to have such a fantastic service, but to be able to offer it as a platform for other companies to use as their own "interactive meeting service" is fantastic. Each partner becomes an ambassador and the recurring revenues generated from licenses and usage should grow fast over the next decade.

Interactive Network

WebEx also has an intensive server network to handle its customer load. WebEx's Interactive Network (WIN) is a globally distributed network designed to execute services through WebEx hubs. This network includes high capacity Internet connections via multiple dedicated leased lines. There are more than 120 WebEx servers in six data centers across the U.S., Europe, and Asia.

Competition

WebEx has many companies that try to compete in the virtual meeting market, but there are only three primary competitors:

- Centra (CTRA), www.centra.com, Lexington, MA
- PlaceWare (private), www.placeware.com, Mountain View, CA
- Evoke (EVOK), www.evoke.com, Louisville, CO

Some might say that Microsoft Net Meeting might also be a player in this market. It's a great product, but it's very limited compared to WebEx. This is a point-to-point product and after adding a third or more parties, the application is not reliable. There also seems to be a potential firewall problem according to several sources. Another application that is very similar is Sametime, which is a Lotus product.

- Microsoft's Net Meeting (MSFT), www.microsoft.com/windows/netmeeting, Redmond, WA
- Lotus Development's Sametime, www.lotus.com, Cambridge, MA, subsidiary of IBM

There are many other companies who claim to be competitors, but they have a long way to go to really compete with WebEx.

- Interwise (private), www.interwise.com, Santa Clara, CA
- Mentergy (private, was LearnLinc), www.mentergy.com, New York City
- Pixion's Picturetalk (private), www.pixion.com, Pleasanton, CA
- HorizonLive (private), www.horizonlive.com, New York City
- Latitude (LATD), www.latitude.com, Santa Clara, CA, (Focused on intra-company use)
- Compac's Carbon Copy (CPQ), (like PC Anywhere), Houston, TX
- Symantec's PC Anywhere (SYMC), www.symantec.com, Cupertino, CA

There are also many small players offering Internet voice over IP, but these are very restrictive in terms of service and features. Spiderphone is a good example.

What makes this product/service unique?

WebEx has one huge strategic advantage over its competition. All three of WebEx's primary competitors use "store-and-forward" technology versus WebEx's "information switch-based network" architecture. In basic terms, store-and-forward technology is server-database driven and is therefore limited in its security, resolution, functionality, scalability, and, most importantly, its reliability. WebEx's information-switching platform has very few limitations because it works like voice-switching platforms in the telephony world, where you have a network of switches that deliver real-time voice, presentations, documents, and any application including video or web pages.

In essence, comparing store-and-forward technology to a information switched-based network is like comparing a phone conversation to e-mail. One is switch-based, scalable (two or many people can participate) and real-time with no download. The other requires a server from which the data is retrieved. With store-and-forward technology, the application or document that is being shared must be downloaded from the server in the middle to the participants, which is time-consuming and not as practical. WebEx's distributed network architecture uses T120 data-conferencing technology to immediately view the meeting leader's screen so there is no downloading of shared files. The meeting is conducted seamlessly in real time. What's also unique about WebEx's technology is their ability to offer remote control—where any participant, with permission, can take control of the leader's computer.

It would make sense that as technology advances (and the competition gets smarter), the competition may soon be adopting this "web-ready" format, which may eliminate WebEx's one strategic advantage. However, by then WebEx should have a huge lead in the industry.

One other difference between Centra Software and WebEx is focus. Centra is a fantastic company and the best investment alternative to WebEx. They have "Centra eMeeting" and "Centra Conference" that are direct competitors. They also have "Centra Symposium," which is an eLearning tool for synchronous learning that many other eLearning companies are using as part of their platform. However, the number one problem with this competitor is their divided focus. They may be the leader in the virtual-classroom market, but they are second to WebEx in the virtual-meeting (web-conferencing) market.

WebEx's proprietary technology is also firewall-friendly, which means their service has very little problem being used by companies that have robust firewalls that protect the company from outside computer hackers. Almost all of the competitors do not have this advantage.

WebEx's remote control feature is also unique and not offered by their primary competitors. This feature is very competitive with Symantec's PC Anywhere, which also allows sharing of control over the web. However, PC Anywhere is "client-to-client" technology, which means it only works one on one. WebEx allows anyone in the meeting to do this because it uses technology known as T120 protocol and TCP/IP ports.

WebEx also uses Vector Based Graphics that give documents and slides much higher resolution than most of their competitors.

With other web-conferencing companies, one can't save or print (unless it's a print screen) any of the annotations that were made to a shared document. WebEx's portable format allows a person to print and save the documents with annotations. How? It's not the actual document file that's being shared. It's a shared PDF (portable document format) with annotations.

WebEx's Interactive Network is very unique and proof of their commitment to being the leader in this industry.

Finally, WebEx has big plans for the future. They want to be the standard in the real time web meeting market. WebEx wants to create an interface that will enable real time communications on any web site or application. Application Program Interface is the way a computer application program makes requests of the operating system or another application. This will make it easy for developers to incorporate WebEx's interactive communications platform into web sites or software applications. Having WebEx as the web meeting "dial tone" means that any web site could become an on-line meeting environment.

Partners/alliances

WebEx has many partners within several different categories as mentioned earlier in this chapter. Other partners include: Peachtree, PaloAlto Software, Yellowpages.com, Done.com, FatJob.com, InvestorForce.com, Partnerwise, CoCounselor.com, Marketing Central, EnergyPrism.com, V2Commerce, Ulearn.com, Net2Phone.com, Lucent, Primus, MindCrossing, and Kingsstad.

Conclusion

WebEx has carved out an incredible niche and their competitors are close behind, fighting to provide competitive features and services. However, with the momentum behind WebEx, it may take them a while. WebEx has a strategic advantage that will be hard to beat.

WebEx
NASDAQ Symbol: WEBX
100 Rose Orchard Way
San Jose, CA 95134
408-435-7284
CEO Subrah S. Iyar
Web Site www.webex.com

Genomics
Research Content

PE Corp Celera Genomics

Biotechnology and Genomics
What is a Genome?

The genome contains all the genetic material that makes up an organism. For example, the human genome is the digital genetic "codebook" for a human being. (The "book" analogy is from Matt Ridley, *Genome: The Autobiography of a Species in 23 Chapters,* HarperCollins, 1999). The human body contains roughly 100 trillion (100 x 10^{12}) cells. Inside the nucleus of each cell are two complete sets of the human genome—one from the father and one from the mother. The code is written entirely in three-letter words, using four chemical letters (bases): A, C, G, and T (adenine, cytosine, guanine, and thymine). The codebook for the human genome has over one billion words. The three billion letters of text would fill a stack of paper 150 feet high.

It's important to note that the genome is written linearly, in one dimension and one direction. It's a sequence of letters as opposed to a blueprint (which many people use as an analogy for the genome), which is two-dimensional. The genome is written on long chains of sugar and phosphate called DNA molecules. Each of the twenty-three human chromosomes is one pair of long DNA molecules. Each chromosome employs several thousand genes.

The purpose of a gene is to store the recipe for making proteins. These proteins do almost every chemical, structural, and regulatory thing that is done in the body: they generate energy, fight infection, digest food, form hair, carry oxygen, and so on and on. Every single protein in the body is made from a gene by a translation of the genetic code. What's interesting about genes is that they are like chunks of software that can run on any system, even in other organisms. They use the same code to do the same jobs.

A great way to learn more about biotechnology and genomics is to go to www.celera.com, select "Celera Science" and click on their "Genomics Education" button. Here you can view a number of basic short classes on DNA, chromosomes, drugs, and drug targets. We urge you to take advantage of this fantastic feature on Celera's site.

History

It all started in the 1860s when Gregor Mendel, an Augustinian friar, was studying pea plants and how certain characteristics were inherited from other parent plants. In the 1940s, Oswald Avery and his associates were working with bacteria, and they discovered that it was the DNA molecule that carried the genetic material, (not the proteins as previously thought). In 1953, the double helix model of DNA was developed by James D. Watson and Francis H.C. Crick.

The term biotechnology refers to the use of microorganisms, such as bacteria, or biological substances like enzymes, to perform specific tasks. The tasks we are referring to in this book specifically involve the cure or prevention of a disease. Biotechnology as an industry was born when the U.S. government and the National Cancer Institute (NCI) decided to attack cancer in the 1970s by spending hundreds of millions of dollars on biotechnology research.

In 1980, biotech's first initial public offering, Genentech, made the business of biotechnology real. Plus, the U.S. Supreme Court ruled in *Diamond v. Chakrabarty* that genetically engineered organisms can be patented, which empowered biotech companies to protect their discoveries and inventions. By 1985, Genentech had produced the world's first biotech product, the recombinant human-growth hormone. It was then that the Human Genome Project began, which was coordinated by the U.S. Department of Energy and the National Institutes of Health.

The first complete copy of the human genome was mapped and sequenced in the United States by PE CORP—Celera Genomics and simultaneously by the U.S. Human Genome Project on June 26, 2000. This changed the world. This mapping of the genome suddenly gives us an opportunity to fully understand the human genetic code. This is truly revolutionary. We have a great deal of new answers, but many new questions as well.

The basic goal of both parties behind mapping the genome was to:

- Identify all of the 100,000 genes in human DNA
- Determine the sequences of the three billion chemical pairs in the DNA
- Save this information in a database
- Design software tools for data analysis
- Offer these related technologies to others

The biggest commercial focus for biotech research is cancer treatment. The dream of most biotech investors has been to own these so-called anti-cancer stocks. Traditionally, the anti-cancer biopharmaceutical companies concentrated on developing new chemotherapy drugs and pursuing cancer vaccines. "Big pharma" (large pharmaceutical companies) was reluctant to accept the idea that it might be off course in trying to develop silver-bullet cancer killers. Because of their huge profit potential, the push for new chemotherapy drugs and cancer vaccines remains very strong. The long-term bets should, however, be on antibody companies (which are close to profitable success) and gene-therapy companies (which are further out). Why? It can be argued that all disease is genetic. Paul Berg, inventor of genetic engineering and Nobel laureate, once wrote, "I start with the premise that all diseases are genetic." Therefore, the key lies in the genome, and big pharma might miss the boat.

In regard to the future as an investor, it's important to note that many of these smaller genomic companies have the potential to be purchased by big pharma or biotech companies. Most of the larger companies have a huge appetite for smaller entities that are pending FDA approval or have FDA approval. Instead of pouring hundreds of millions of dollars into genomic research, the bigger pharmaceutical and biotech companies let the little guys fight it out, spend their investors' money, and just buy the winners. This is a low-risk way for the larger companies to build their product offering.

Future of the sector

There is a huge amount of promise lying in the future of the genomic industry. Cures for so many genetic mistakes, like cancer and cystic fibrosis, could be only a few years away. The following vignettes illustrate the possibilities:

> A woman with breast cancer is able to take a revolutionary drug that completely eliminates the cancerous cells and leaves her healthy and strong with no chemotherapy or surgery.

> A man suffering from Alzheimer's disease for years is given treatment and within days, he's able to connect emotionally and mentally with his family again.

> A woman suffering from an inherited predisposition to heart disease is diagnosed, treated, and lives to be over 100.

Next are two more examples of what the biotech/genomics industry could bring us in the future:

> The space station is now self-sufficient with crops that produce enough food to feed the entire crew.

> A spacecraft lands on Mars with cellular-like material carrying genetic-encoded information that learns to evolve into a living organism that can survive on the planet. This organism quickly evolves and completely changes the environment, making it possible for humans to live there.

Market potential

When you are talking about revolutionizing the world of pharmaceuticals, creating cures for genetic mistakes, and sending cellular material to Mars capable of building an environment for humans, it is impossible to estimate the potential market. Many of these companies try to target certain areas of disease or genetic mistakes, and while that might be easy to estimate in terms of market potential, as far as this industry as a whole, it is impossible to imagine because the applications are so broad.

J. Craig Venter, Ph.D., president and chief scientific officer of Celera Genomics, said in its 1999 annual report, "[T]he level of annual spending in the U.S. biomedical research market alone is valued at $40 billion annually, and global markets in drug discovery, drug development, diagnostics, and agriculture are valued at an additional $44 billion annually." It's our belief that this industry has the potential to grow at high double-digit rates.

How is this sector changing the world?

The biotech and genomic industries have already changed the pharmaceutical industry by changing the focus of drug development more toward science and discovery. When Genentech was founded, they had no marketing experience. All they had was the science of biotechnology and a focus on finding cures and preventative medicines that could revolutionize the drug industry. It was their belief that if they built the cures, the business would come.

When the human genome was mapped, the world was given a blueprint of the genetic makeup of humans, opening the door for genomics as an industry and gene therapy as a real treatment. Suddenly the pace of drug development is speeding up—some industry experts say as much as five times faster. Matt Ridley, in his book, *Genome: The Autobiography of a Species* said, "Compared with the knowledge to be gleaned from the genome, the whole of the rest of biology is but a thimbleful." (Ridley, pp. 61-62)

What is really fascinating about this industry is what we call the David and Goliath Effect. It is when a small company comes up with a breakthrough discovery that revolutionizes a niche industry with a proprietary product, license, or patent, which makes the current established company's products obsolete. The potential is there for a small biotech/genomic company to produce a product that cures arthritis, making all other arthritis drugs obsolete. Genomics and biotechnology have the potential to single handedly change almost every facet of medicine and biology from cancer to space exploration.

Structure of this Industry

There are approximately three hundred biotech/genomic companies that are public today and only about twenty of them have positive cash flow. The leaders include:

- Amgen (AMGN)
- Genentech (DNA)
- Immunex (IMNX)
- Biogen (BGEN)

The top ten companies in the biotech industry make up approximately 90% of the capitalization of the entire industry. In other words, the biggest companies control most of the industry.

The leaders in genomic research and drug development include:

- Celera Genomics
  www.celera.com
- Millennium Pharmaceuticals
  www.mlnm.com
- Affymetrix (AFFX)
  www.affymetrix.com
- Human Genome Science (HGSI)
  www.hgsi.com
- Incyte Genomics, Inc. (INCY)
  www.incyte.com
- Curagen Corporation (CRGN)
  www.curagen.com
- Gene Logic, Inc. (GLGC)
  www.genelogic.com
- Myriad Genetics (MYGN)
  www.myriad.com
- Lynx Therapeutics, Inc. (LYNX)
  www.lynxgen.com
- Genome Therapeutics (GENE)
  www.cric.com

This industry is growing so fast that by the time this is read, there will certainly be many more companies that have gone public. It's estimated that over 1,000 biotech/genomic companies are private. Many are planning to go public in the next six months.

Investing in Biotechnology Companies

Morningstar (10/31/2000) reports financial results for 230 listed biotechnology companies.

- 27 (12%) of these firms report no current revenue.
- 38 (17%) of these firms report *positive* current income.
- The largest firm, Amgen, has a market capitalization of $59.6 billion.
- The smallest firm, Applied Biometrics, has a market capitalization of $1 million.
- The median in the sample, Bone Care International, has a market capitalization of $282 million.
- 42 firms (18%) have market capitalizations greater than $1 billion—(82% are *less than* $1 billion).
- 70 firms (30%) are classified as *distressed.*
- Quintiles Transnational has the largest number of employees, 20,453; the median number of employees for all 230 companies is 86; only 27 firms (12%) have more than 500 employees.

Nonetheless:

- 78 companies had YTD market returns greater than 50%.
- 61 companies had YTD market returns greater than 75%.
- 50 companies had YTD market returns greater than 100%.
- 23 companies had YTD market returns greater than 200%.

Source: www.Morningstar.com

Conclusion

The biggest risk for the investor when selecting a genomic company is owning a stock that has only one or two different drugs in the development stage. Genomics is an emerging industry with at least a two-year time horizon before a gene-therapy drug is approved by the FDA. Therefore, all genomic drugs are in the development and testing stage. The expenses related to development and testing can run in the hundreds of millions of dollars. Therefore, very few companies have the resources to focus on more than one drug.

We've selected two genomic companies, both of which have unique platform-type offerings. Celera has a database platform that could be the greatest biotech library in the world. Millennium has a process platform that has the potential to be the equivalent of the Microsoft Office™ of biotechnology.

It's important to note that although Celera has their own fantastic process platform that integrates all their data and analysis tools, their core competency and strategic advantage lies in their databases of genomic information.

PE Corp Celera Genomics
Company Description

Deriving its name from the Latin word for swiftness, Celera was formed for the purpose of generating genomic information to accelerate the understanding of biological processes. Celera Genomics was established in May 1998 by the PE Corporation and J. Craig Venter, Ph.D., a leading genomic scientist and founder of The Institute for Genomic Research.

Celera's goal is to be the world's definitive source of genomic and related medical and agricultural information. It plans to do this by identifying and making genomic data (a data platform) available to researchers, while simultaneously providing a new approach to pharmaceutical development (a process platform). The first could change the world's understanding of disease, and the second the world of pharmaceutical development by making it more systematic and less random.

Celera wants to change the way physicians diagnose a patient's disease. Instead of basing the diagnosis on symptoms, it wants to base it on the patient's genetic components, thereby creating a new kind of medical practice that is more preventative and better at treating existing disease.

Company History

In 1998, Celera Genomics consisted of only a handful of people and an almost impossible goal. That goal was to become the world's definitive source of genomic and related agricultural and medical information. Today the company is well on its way. Below, we've mapped out the somewhat confusing origin of Celera and its relationship to PE Corp, which is now Applera.

In 1993, The Perkin-Elmer Corporation of Norwalk, Connecticut, merged with Applied Biosystems, Inc., which was founded in Foster City, California, in 1981. In 1998, Perkin-Elmer consolidated its premier life-science technologies into the PE Biosystems division, consisting of Applied Biosystems, PerSeptive Biosystems, Tropix, and PE Informatics.

In order to focus its mission on the life sciences, the company was recapitalized under the name PE Corporation in 1999. As part of the recapitalization, the company established two new classes of common stock that track the Applied Biosystems Group (PE Biosystems Group) and the Celera Genomics Group (PE Corp Celera). The company also sold its analytical instruments division and the Perkin-Elmer name, which was most closely associated with that business.

The Applied Biosystems Group develops and markets instrument-based systems, reagents, software, and contract services to the life-science industry and research community. Customers use these tools to analyze nucleic acids (DNA and RNA), small molecules, and proteins in order to make scientific discoveries, develop new pharmaceuticals, and conduct standardized testing.

As of November 30, 2000, PE Corp became Applera and its stock symbol on the New York Stock Exchange (NYSE) changed from PEB to ABI. This new name is a combination of the names of the company's two operating businesses, the Applied Biosystems Group and the Celera Genomics Group. Celera's headquarters are located in Rockville, Maryland. Celera's DNA sequencing factory, comprising 300 ABI PRISM® 3700 DNA Analyzers from PE Biosystems, is the world's largest.

Description of product/service

Celera's key product is their genomic information or databases that help other facilities to pursue and concentrate on identifying disease-causing genes, achieve new medical discoveries, reconsider untreatable disorders, and take a more systematic approach to drug design. Celera accomplishes their mission using four platforms:

- Celera Discovery System™
- Celera Genome Reference Database
- Celera SNP Reference Database
- Celera Services

Celera Discovery System™ (CDS) is the company's new biomedical discovery platform for genomic research and drug discovery, which is designed to speed up the discovery process. This is a web-based portal through which a variety of customers access Celera's expanding databases and analysis tools. This platform of tools should enable their customers and future partners to more efficiently manage and analyze the large volumes of biological and medical data, making it easier to create new and better-targeted drugs, as well as new diagnostic products.

Celera Genome Reference Database includes the human genome-mapping database that made Celera famous. This database is the key to understanding normal physiology and mechanisms of disease. The components include databases of human genome data, as well as Drosophila (fruit fly), and mouse genomes that have been sequenced (mapped/cataloged) by Celera. These databases are completely integrated with twenty other third-party reference databases, along with a suite of analysis tools, thus creating one of the greatest biotech libraries to date.

Celera SNP Reference Database is a comprehensive collection of documented variations in the genomes that have been computed and validated in Celera's efforts, as well as other public efforts. SNP or Single Nucleotide Polymorphisms are the major form of DNA variation responsible for human traits, certain illnesses, and variable drug safety and efficacy. A central part of the Celera Genomics mission is to identify and catalog these single-letter DNA variations or SNPs. Current research indicates that individual genomes differ by more than one million base pairs.

These SNPs, for example, are used to identify the differentiating characteristics between normal genetic data and genetic mistakes, permitting researchers to discover improved drug therapies.

Celera Services include the rest of Celera's platform of services that centers around their GeneTag™ process, allowing researchers to take separate unorganized DNA fragments and match them with their corresponding gene names. Celera Service also includes Global Gene Expression Profiling, Gene Discovery, and Industrial-Grade Genomics, all of which compliment the other services.

All of these services involve recurring license fees and subscription fees from their clients and subscribers.

Why is there a need for their service?

As you may know, some drugs work well in some patients while being virtually useless or even harmful in others. In fact, some are fatal—approximately 100,000 people die each year in the U.S. due to pharmaceutical-drug side effects. This is because today's drugs are not tailored to each individual. They are mass-produced. What if a doctor could prescribe medicines tailored to the genetic profile of individual patients? If Celera is successful in their mission, tomorrow's drugs will be specifically tailored and designed for individual genetic profiles, so that adverse reactions become a thing of the past.

Competition

In terms of Celera's database, there is no real competition. Therefore, the only real competition would be the other genomic companies listed above in the genomic industry section.

What makes Celera Unique?

This company is unique because of its database of genomic information (the mapping of genomes) for humans and other organisms. Celera's database is its strategic advantage, but the way it is organized and offered to the world of pharmaceutical research makes the advantage even greater. It would be almost impossible for another firm to catch up with them.

Celera's use of technology has helped it take the lead in discovery and management of genomic information. For example, the assembly of a bacterial genome that took eleven days in 1996 took just over five minutes in early 1999.

Celera's management team seems to be a hard driving, outspoken machine capable of achieving the impossible. Their leader, J. Craig Venter, Ph.D., president and chief scientific officer, has assembled a world-class scientific, technical, and management team to help the company quickly achieve its goals. Almost all of the key leadership are either a Ph.D. or M.D., and they are some of the world's foremost experts in genomic sequencing, computing, software design, and informatics.

"In just over two years since its inception, Celera has made incredible strides in building the definitive reference source of genomic information. We are moving forward on a broad front to establish a biomedical discovery platform," said Tony L. White, PE Corporation's chief executive officer. "We intend to leverage our scientific platforms and capabilities to make discoveries that enable our customers and future partners to create new and better targeted drugs, as well as new diagnostic products. We are beginning to assemble a subscriber base of leading academic institutions and pharmaceutical and agricultural companies who see the extraordinary value of our information and partnership services." (Celera's 1999 annual report)

Strategic Alliances

Charter genomic database subscribers include: Amgen, Novartis, Pharmacia, and Upjohn. As early-access partners with five-year subscriptions to Celera's information, these pharmaceutical leaders are able to offer input into the development of Celera's software tools and genomic databases. Early-access subscriptions include associated bioinformatics systems and tools for viewing, browsing, and analyzing genomic information. Bioinformatics is the science of developing computer databases and algorithms for the purpose of speeding up and enhancing biological research.

RhoBio Agreement

This three-year agreement with RhoBio S.A., a joint venture of Rhone-Poulenc Agro and Biogemma, will use expression studies to discover genes related to traits of importance in maize. Celera AgGen will receive royalties from RhoBio resulting from sales of any products developed through this research-based alliance.

Rhone-Poulenc Rohrer (RPR) Alliance

Celera and RPR launched a three-year gene-discovery agreement to identify therapeutic targets for a variety of human diseases, including asthma, cancer, and cardiovascular disorders. RPR will apply Celera's proprietary GeneTag™ technology to its disease model systems.

LION bioscience AG

Most recently (November 9, 2000), Celera Genomics and LION bioscience AG (Neuer Markt: LIO; NASDAQ: LEON) announced that they have extended their existing collaboration and have entered into a new strategic alliance to develop and deliver new software tools through the Celera Discovery System™ (CDS). Celera and LION will collaborate to create improved software tools to meet the dynamic bioinformatics needs of life-science researchers. Under the agreement, the two companies intend to further develop and customize the LION SRS system to better organize and analyze the large volume of new biological data being created by Celera and others. They also intend to develop new technologies to couple premier analysis tools with the most extensive collection of genomic and biological data. In addition, Celera will offer LION's automated genome annotation, comparison and expression analysis tools, bioSCOUT®, genomeSCOUT™, and arraySCOUT™, through the CDS.

Other Alliances

Celera entered into subscription agreements with the Weizmann Institute of Science in Israel, the California Institute of Technology, and The Institute for Genomic Research that grant access to certain of Celera's information through the Celera Discovery System.

In addition, the Howard Hughes Medical Institute reached an agreement with Celera to purchase access to the group's comprehensive reference libraries.

Valigen N.V., a European-American functional genomics company, entered into an agreement with Celera that provides access to all of Celera's integrated database products, bioinformatics systems, and other discovery tools.

Celera depends a great deal upon the sequencing breakthrough of the ABI PRISM® 3700 DNA Analyzer and other leading technologies from PE Biosystems, and the support of their computing and database partners, Compaq and Oracle.

Conclusion

J. Craig Venter, Ph.D., said in Celera's 1999 annual report, "As the genomic age takes hold across life sciences, we believe that as-yet-unimagined paradigms and disciplines around gene regulation and gene networks will begin to appear. I find it appealing that as the next millennium dawns, Celera is helping to launch a new era that will have fundamental implications for the quality of our lives. Over the next year, we will continue building our databases and refining our Internet-based information delivery to make this new age a reality. We will also increase our customer base to build revenue. Considering that, the business opportunities for Celera are as impressive as the biomedical and agricultural breakthroughs are likely to be."

With the momentum behind their successful databases and their big-picture leadership, this company should withstand the volatility and risks associated with biotech and genomic research and development and continue to be a market leader decades from now.

Celera: PE Corporation
NASDAQ Symbol: CRA
761 Main Avenue
Norwalk, Connecticut 06859-0001
(203) 762-1000 / (800) 761-5381
CEO J. Craig Venter, Ph.D.
Web Site www.celera.com

Genomic
Drug Development
Millennium Pharmaceuticals

Genomics and Millennium

The previous chapter gave a brief explanation of biotechnology and genomics. We've selected another genomic company, Millennium, that we feel complements Celera and its database platform. Therefore, it's important to know that these two companies, in our view, do not compete.

Our goal in genomics, as with all the other industries, was to find the platforms that other firms would use or partner with. We wanted to reduce our risk by finding a company that either provided the platform for other larger pharmaceutical companies interested in genomics or the company that was smart enough to partner with these larger companies. Millennium Pharmaceuticals does both. Through its platform, it partners with other companies to research and produce gene-therapy applications.

We've selected Millennium Pharmaceuticals because it provides a series of research platforms that help the company partner with many different firms, thus diversifying its product mix and risk.

Millennium Pharmaceuticals
Company Description

Millennium Pharmaceuticals wants to be the Biopharmaceutical Company of the Future. As their CEO, Mark Levin's goal is to "fundamentally change the practice of medicine as we know it today."

Millennium's focus is to develop drugs that cure and prevent diseases and genetic mistakes in three areas: oncology, inflammation, and metabolic disease. It is the company's belief that by understanding the relationship between genes and diseases, it can "deliver precisely the right medicine to precisely the right patient at precisely the right time."

Its strategy is not just to develop drugs, but also to develop and constantly improve proprietary platforms (research and drug development processes) that optimize every step of their work.

Currently, these platforms are used to form strategic alliances with larger pharmaceutical companies. However, Millennium's goal is to use these same platforms to partner with patients, physicians, academics, and health-care providers. It plans to facilitate this with other partners such as software providers, instrument makers, and Internet companies.

Millennium currently has over 1,400 U.S. and foreign patents and patent applications, of which 119 are actual issued U.S. patents in force today. These include drug-discovery methods, genes they've identified, and their medical uses.

Company History

The company was started in 1993 as a drug-discovery and development company. It is located in Cambridge, Massachusetts, near top colleges such as MIT and Harvard. Millennium's potential for growth and strong reputation have attracted some very accomplished talent from around the world. Currently, it has over 1,000 employees.

Description of product/service

Millennium has many different drugs in several different phases of development. Melastatin™, which is a gene used in a molecular diagnostic test that describes a patient's current medical condition and provides prognostic and therapeutic information, is currently pending commercialization. For example, detecting Melastatin in patient-tissue samples can determine whether a patient has or is at risk of developing metastatic melanoma, a serious form of skin cancer.

Awaiting FDA approval is CAMPATH®, an oncology therapeutic candidate for the treatment of chronic lymphocytic leukemia, the most pervasive adult form of leukemia.

Millennium also has two candidates in clinical trials for oncology:

- CAMPATH® Phase I & II for other oncology indications
- LDP-341 Phase I for solid tumors and hematological malignancies

(Please note: Phases I, II, and III are the clinical testing phases within the seven step process of attaining FDA Approval. The seven steps are: Preclinical Testing; Investigational New Drug application (IND); Clinical Testing Phases I, II, & III; New Drug Application (NDA); and finally the Approval Phase.)

In the clinical pipeline, Millennium has four candidates in clinical trials for inflammation:

- LDP-02, Phase II trials for Chrohn's disease and ulcerative colitis
- LDP-519, Phase I for stroke and myocardial infarction
- LDP-01, Phase I for prevention of post-ischemic reperfusion injury
- LDP-977, Phase II for asthma

In the preclinical pipeline, there are candidates for all three of its franchise areas, including rheumatoid arthritis, allergic hypersensitivity, HIV, restenosis, immune suppression, juvenile onset diabetes, transplantation, atopic dermatitis, obesity, cancer cachexia, and anorexia. Like most genomic or biotech firms, Millennium's primary product would seem to be the drugs they are working to develop. However, there is more to the company than drugs; it's their platform that fascinates us.

Millennium has developed a series of proprietary platforms it uses to optimize every step of the drug-discovery process from identifying the gene to clinical tests and product manufacturing. This platform keeps Millennium and its partners from "reinventing the wheel" each time it sets out to do research or develop a drug. The process of research and drug development is very complicated and involves huge amounts of data. Anything that improves this process gives genomic companies a big advantage over their competition. Their science and technology platforms together empower them and their partners to develop drugs faster and more efficiently with less capital by integrating all the necessary elements. These elements include genomics, chemistry, and even robotics.

More specifically, they use such tools as microchip formats that require very little sample material and highly automated proprietary processes and software to analyze DNA sequence. The goal here is to optimize the process of developing world-changing therapeutic and predictive medicines. This comprehensive platform has four tiers:

- Identify genes
- Elucidate their function
- Validate targets
- Develop products

Competition

There are two ways to look at competition for Millennium. First, it has three primary drug therapy focuses, which are oncology, inflammation, and metabolic disease. There are a number of competing companies in those areas. Secondly, however, the company's proprietary platform and its use in setting up strategic alliances have very little, if any, competition. Millennium's key competition today would be the other genomic companies, but soon it may be the larger biotech companies. Our bet is that Millennium will eventually be their biggest competition or their most important strategic alliance.

What makes this product/service unique?

Millennium's vision is to be the "Biopharmaceutical Company of the Future." This vision alone makes it remarkable. The company seems to see a bigger picture than most of its competition. Management's focus on changing the world is key to their success. Their platforms clearly make them the leader in the industry. These platforms allow them to leverage their abilities with other, larger firms to produce recurring revenue streams for years.

Millennium's focus on partnerships is an almost never-ending source of revenue and investment for the company. Its committed focus on three areas is also attractive. By focusing on the core competencies, the company has a better chance of being the best.

Strategic Alliances and Partners

To understand the depth of this company, the depth of their strategic alliances must be understood. Here we've listed, from its web site, each of the largest strategic alliances Millennium has currently. Millennium has three types of alliances or partnerships:

- Drug Development Partners/alliances
- Technology Partnerships
- Millennium's Predictive Medicine, Inc. (MPMx) Collaborations

Drug Development Partners/alliances

The following is a list of current partnerships with other companies that utilize Millennium's platforms for drug development. (Taken from www.celera.com)

AHP (American Home Products) /Wyeth-Ayerst: Antibacterial

Through its acquisition of ChemGenics in February 1997, Millennium became engaged in a strategic alliance with American Home Products Corporation (AHP) to discover novel drug leads for the treatment of bacterial infections in humans. Under the terms of the alliance, which is valued at $20 million excluding milestones and royalties, AHP is funding and collaborating with Millennium on a five-year program of antibacterial research. The alliance was extended for two additional years in October 1999. Millennium received nine milestone payments from Wyeth-Ayerst for the acceptance of nine antibacterial drug targets into screening. Additionally, Millennium has received bonus payments for delivering multiple drug targets in the first two years of the alliance.

AHP/Wyeth-Ayerst: CNS

In July 1996, Millennium entered into a strategic alliance with AHP to discover and develop targets and assays to identify small molecule drugs and vaccines for the treatment and prevention of disorders of the central nervous system (CNS). The strategic alliance (valued at $90 million excluding milestones and royalties) with AHP consists of three major components: CNS disease drug-discovery research, informatics technology and support and technology exchange. This alliance was extended for at least two additional years in August 1999.

Aventis Pharma

In June 2000, Millennium and Aventis Pharma, the pharmaceutical company of Aventis S.A., formed an alliance to identify drug targets, develop new drugs in the field of inflammation, and jointly commercialize the resulting products in North America. Under the agreement, the two companies will also jointly develop new drug-discovery technologies. In return for a total investment of $450 million, including payments of up to $200 million over five years and a $250 million equity investment, Aventis will receive access to key elements of Millennium's technology platform. The primary goal of the inflammation collaboration is to jointly discover, develop, and commercialize products to treat specific inflammatory diseases: rheumatoid arthritis, asthma and chronic obstructive pulmonary disease, multiple sclerosis, and inflammatory bowel disease.

Bayer AG

In September 1998, Millennium and Bayer AG formed an alliance believed to be the largest in the field of pharmaceutical research. In return for a total investment of $465 million, including approximately a 14% equity investment in Millennium, Bayer AG will receive access to key technologies in modern genome research and a flow of new genomics-based targets for drug development over a five-year period. The primary goal of the alliance is for Millennium to supply 225 important new "drug targets" to Bayer AG that are identified as relevant for cardiovascular disease, cancer, osteoporosis, pain, liver fibrosis, hematology, and viral infections. Those targets identified and validated by Millennium will be screened by Bayer AG.

Eli Lilly and Company

In October 1995, Millennium and Eli Lilly and Company (Lilly) entered into a strategic alliance in the field of atherosclerosis valued at $41 million (excluding milestones and royalties). At the same time, Lilly made an $8 million equity investment in Millennium. In September 1997, Lilly and Millennium expanded the scope of the program to include congestive heart failure. This part of the program was extended for an additional year in June 2000.

In April 1996, Millennium and Lilly entered into a strategic alliance in select areas within oncology valued at $28 million (excluding milestones and royalties). This agreement was renewed for two additional years in January 1999.

Millennium received a milestone payment when Lilly accepted an atherosclerosis target into screening and three additional payments when Lilly accepted two prostate cancer drug-candidate genes and one drug-resistance gene for use in the development of small molecule therapeutics.

Genentech, Inc.

Through its merger with LeukoSite in December 1999, Millennium joined Genentech in a collaborative agreement. This agreement, established in 1997, is focused on the development and commercialization of LDP-02, a humanized monoclonal antibody for the treatment of inflammatory bowel disease (IBD). Genentech's support of the program, including an equity investment, a credit facility and milestone payments, could reach approximately $50 million, excluding royalties and profit sharing.

ILEX Oncology and Schering AG/Berlex Labs

In August 1999, LeukoSite, Inc., ILEX Oncology, Inc., and Schering AG entered into a distribution and development agreement that grants Schering AG exclusive marketing and distribution rights to CAMPATH® in the U.S., Europe and the rest of the world, except Japan and East Asia. CAMPATH® is a humanized monoclonal antibody in late-stage development. Following the merger of Millennium and LeukoSite in December 1999, Millennium and ILEX have retained rights to CAMPATH® in

Japan and East Asia. Millennium and ILEX have submitted a Biologics License Application (BLA) for CAMPATH® with the U.S. Food and Drug Administration (FDA).

Kyowa Hakko Kogyo Co., Ltd.

Through its merger with LeukoSite in December 1999, Millennium joined Kyowa Hakko Kogyo in a discovery and development collaboration. Under this agreement, Kyowa Hakko Kogyo provides Millennium with scientific and financial resources for the application of chemokine receptor technology to the discovery of new treatments for inflammatory and autoimmune diseases. In addition to research funding and milestone payments, Millennium will also receive licensing fees and royalties on worldwide product sales of any products that result from this collaboration. Originally established in 1997, the existing alliance was extended for an additional year in April 2000.

Pfizer Inc.

Through the acquisition of ChemGenics in February 1997, Millennium became engaged in a strategic alliance with Pfizer Inc. to discover novel drug leads for treating fungal infections in humans. Under the terms of the alliance, valued at $24 million (excluding milestones and royalties), Pfizer is funding and collaborating with Millennium on a four-year program of anti-fungal research. Originally due to conclude in December 1999, Pfizer extended the agreement for two additional years. Milestone payments to Millennium are expected to commence with IND filing. Based on significant progress in the fungal collaboration, Pfizer agreed to expand the scope of the program in January 1999 for an additional two years. Additional research personnel were added to the effort.

Roche Bioscience

Millennium maintains a research alliance with Roche Bioscience to develop a small molecule drug for the treatment of patients with asthma and allergic disorders. Under the agreement, Millennium receives licensing fees, research and milestone payments, and royalties on the sale of products resulting from the collaboration.

Taisho Pharmaceutical Co., Ltd.

In January 2000, Millennium and Taisho Pharmaceutical Co., Ltd., announced a development partnership for LDP-977, an investigational drug for the potential treatment of chronic asthma. Under the agreement, Taisho will hold an exclusive license to LDP-977 in Japan, Asia and Europe while Millennium will retain licensing rights for the rest of the world. Taisho will fund all of the research and development expenses of the compound in Japan and Asia and two-thirds of the expenses in the United States and Europe. In addition, Taisho will pay a licensing fee to Millennium, as well as milestone payments for research and development progress in each of Taisho's licensed territories. Millennium will also receive a supply fee based on net sales of the product in each of Taisho's licensed territories, in exchange for Millennium's manufacture and supply of the product to Taisho.

Warner-Lambert Company

Through its December 1999 merger with LeukoSite, Inc., Millennium became engaged in a collaborative agreement with Warner-Lambert Company to discover, develop and commercialize inflammatory and autoimmune disease drugs from small molecule compounds. The two companies are also collaborating on the discovery of small molecules as possible treatments for AIDS. The agreement between LeukoSite and Warner-Lambert was originally established in November 1994. As part of the agreement, Millennium will receive payments in the form of sponsored research, milestone payments, equity investments, and royalties on sales of products licensed to Warner-Lambert outside of North America. In North America, Millennium, and Warner-Lambert may co-promote products derived from the collaboration.

Technology Partnerships

To realize value from its investment in technology development and to access additional resources for such development, Millennium has agreed to transfer components of its technology platform to its partners as part of particular strategic alliances. The list of partners to which the company has transferred technology includes: Eli Lilly and Company, Astra AB, AHP/Wyeth-Ayerst and Pharmacia Corp.

Millennium's Predictive Medicine, Inc. (MPMx) Collaborations

Millennium created its MPMx subsidiary in late 1997 to use its genomics-based scientific and technology platform for the development of genomic and proteomic based products and services to treat and prevent disease. MPMx is trying to develop a new generation of diagnostics to gain a better understanding of a patient's individual response to therapy and provide custom-designed treatment. Through the MPMx subsidiary, Millennium has partnered with the following companies in an attempt to develop individualized diagnostic information and treatments.

- BD (formerly Becton Dickinson and Company)
- Bristol-Myers Squibb

Conclusion

With Millennium's management strength, proprietary platforms, existing partnerships, drugs in the pipeline, capitalization, leadership, and growth momentum, it is difficult to imagine any other genomic company winning the genomic game.

Millennium Pharmaceuticals, Inc.
NASDAQ Symbol: MLNM
75 Sidney Street
Cambridge, MA 02139
617-679-7000
CEO Mark J. Levin
Web Site www.mlnm.com

An Added Bonus

Larger Companies That Are Changing the World

This part of the book is just a little extra for the reader to use in balancing out the risk in his or her portfolio. A portfolio of the stocks listed in Part II can be very volatile. Here is a list of much larger companies that have longer track records and are relatively less risky and hopefully less volatile. Just like the companies in Part II, each of these companies also provides some type of platform or infrastructure for its industry. Together with the stocks above, you can build a more balanced portfolio. We've given a brief description of each stock so each company's mission is better understood.

The Wireless Web, the Smartphone

Nokia, NOK
Corporate Headquarters in Helsinki, Finland
Nokia, U.S. Headquarters:
6000 Connection Drive
Irving, Texas 75039
(972) 894-5000
CEO Jorma Ollila
Web Site www.nokia.com

Nokia is the world's largest supplier of mobile phones with 29% market share. They also are the most profitable mobile phone manufacturer in the world. As the third generation phone systems are installed around the world, Nokia has a great opportunity to be one of the leading suppliers of the Smartphone, as well as the infrastructure equipment it requires.

Internet Bandwidth, Laser and Wave Division Multiplexing (WDM) Components

JDS Uniphase Corporation, JDSU
210 Baypointe Parkway
San Jose, CA 95134 USA
(408) 434-1800
CEO Jozef Straus, Ph.D.
Web Site www.jdsuniphase.com

JDS Uniphase is the leader in fiber-optic communications compo-nents—the component platform for fiber-optic communications traffic. It provides the broadest portfolio of fiber-optic components and mod-ules in the world. Customers include most major telecom & cable Original Equipment Manufacturers such as Lucent, Nortel, Cisco, Alcatel, and Scientific Atlanta. The company's purchase of SDL Purchase solidifies their market leadership in lasers and other fiber-optic communications components.

On-line Auction Platform as a Secondary Market for Any Item

eBay, EBAY
2145 Hamilton Avenue
San Jose, California 95125
Founder Pierre Omidyar
CEO Meg Whitman
Web Site www.ebay.com

eBay is the leader in on-line auction sites. This company is leading the revolution in secondary market for used goods. Current item list-ings (11/29/00) increased to more than 8 million, representing a 60 percent increase from two months ago. eBay just announced an Application Program Interface that will allow other businesses to con-nect and utilize eBay's auction services, giving businesses all over the world a global store in which to market their goods (surpluses, used items, close-out items, etc). This will allow eBay to be fully integrated into sites all over the Internet. It also allows eBay and its partners to quickly expand their services into new IA technology such as Smartphones.

CDMA Technology Platform for the Third Generation Cellular System

> Qualcomm, QCOM
> 5775 Morehouse Drive
> San Diego, CA 92121
> (858) 587-1121
> CEO Dr. Irwin M. Jacobs
> Web Site www.qualcomm.com

Qualcomm is famous for their CDMA technology, which is the platform that makes cell phones communicate much better and clearer than most other cell systems. Its patented product called Code Division Multiple Access or CDMA is the technology of choice for the new third-generation phone systems that are being installed all over the world. CDMA filters out annoying background noise and interference. It also gives towers more coverage area allowing networks to have much fewer tower sites, saving money for both the cellular provider and user. CDMA enables phones to access the web and requires less power from the cellphone battery. CDMA is designed to be the best in giving users security and privacy. More subscribers can use the same CDMA radio frequency, which again helps save money for both the provider and user. CDMA is also easier and less costly to set up than other systems.

Internet and Wireless Infrastructure, including the Last Mile

> Marconi, plc, MONI
> One Bruton Street
> London W1J 6AQ
> United Kingdom
> CEO Lord Simpson
> Web site www.marconi.com

Marconi provides key technologies, equipment, and services for the Internet, enterprise networks and telecommunications systems. Marconi is also a leader in the Internet's Last Mile, which means bringing high bandwidth connections to homes and businesses. With their DISC*S MX flexible access platform, they can use existing copper connections to offer residential and business users high-speed Internet access that is over 100 times faster than today's voice-band modems. Ideally, the best connection would be to have fiber-optic cable connections directly to each home and business. However, it's just too expensive to bring "fiber to the home" or to run individual, dedicated, fiber-optic links to homes that now have copper. Many service providers are looking at ways of bringing "fiber to the curb," because it involves extending fiber in the carrier network to regional or neighborhood hubs housed in outdoor or underground cabinets next to large residential buildings or developments. These locations can then be outfitted with wireless gear bringing optical bandwidth to individual floors of a building or to groups of homes where no fiber exists, or where many users must share a single fiber connection.

Marconi trades on the NASDAQ as an ADR (American Depository Receipt).

Multiple Platform Innovations in Optics and Telecommunication

Lucent, LU
600 Mountain Ave.
Murray Hill, NJ 07974
(908) 582-8500
CEO Henry B. Schacht
Web Site www.lucent.com

Lucent is a leading global supplier of communications networking equipment, holding strong leadership positions in Internet infrastructure for service providers, optical networking, wireless networks, communications networking support and services, communications integrated circuits, and optoelectronic components. The company is focused on a triple play of optical, data and wireless networking technologies with the software and services to support them. Lucent has about 125,000 employees worldwide—about one-quarter of them based outside the United States—and has offices or distributors in more than ninety countries and territories around the world. Bell Labs, Lucent's world-renowned research and development arm, has a presence in thirty-two countries and has produced eleven Nobel laureates since 1937. Scientists and researchers at Bell Labs receive more than four patents every business day. As a communications software powerhouse, two-thirds of Bell Labs is developing next-generation software and applications. Lucent received 1,153 U.S. patents in 1999, making them ninth on the Patent Office's list of companies.

The company introduced the industry's first high-capacity, all-optical router, called WaveStar™ LambdaRouter. It can direct ten times the traffic of today's Internet in one second.

Personal and Small Business Platform for e-commerce and Virtual Office

Yahoo! Inc., YHOO
3420 Central Expressway
Santa Clara, CA 95051
(408) 731-3300
CEO Tim Koogle
Web Site www.yahoo.com

As the first on-line navigational guide to the web, www.yahoo.com is the leading guide in terms of traffic, advertising, household and business-user reach, and is one of the most recognized brands associated with the Internet. It's free to the user and the company's income is derived from advertisements that are sold based on pages delivered containing banner ads. Jerry Yang, a Taiwanese native raised in San Jose, California, co-created the Yahoo! Internet navigational guide in April 1994 with David Filo and co-founded Yahoo! Inc. in April 1995. Yang has been instrumental in building Yahoo! into the world's most highly trafficked web site and one of the Internet's most recognized brands. Yahoo! has 3,059 employees (as of September 30, 2000) and offers a comprehensive branded network of services to more than 145 million individuals each month worldwide. The company also provides on-line business services designed to enhance the web presence of Yahoo!'s clients, including audio and video streaming, store hosting and management, and web site tools and services. The company's global web network includes twenty-two local world properties outside the United States. With on-line advertising sales growing approximately 150% per year, Yahoo! has the potential to remain the brand name leader in Internet navigation for decades to come.

Second Largest Biotechnology Discovery Platform

Genentech, Inc., DNA
1 DNA Way
South San Francisco, CA 94080-4990
(650) 225-1000
CEO Arthur D. Levinson, Ph. D.
Web Site www.gene.com

Founded in 1976, Genentech, the original pioneer in biotechnology, continues its leadership in the field. They manufacture and market nine protein-based pharmaceuticals, including four different growth-hormone treatments. Those products are Protropin, Nutropin, Nutropin AQ, and Nutropin Depot. The company's five other protein-based pharmaceuticals are Pulmozyme, an inhalation treatment for management of cystic fibrosis; Activase and TNKase for acute myocardial infarction (heart attack); Rituxan, treatment for B-cell non-Hodgkin's lymphoma; and Herceptin, for breast cancer. The company's product pipeline is broad, deep and diverse. They currently have eighteen active projects, fifteen of which are in at least in Phase I, twelve of which are in Phase II—more clinical trials now than any other point in their history. Genentech has over twenty-five partners or strategic alliances that help them access other products and technologies that strengthen their product pipeline. Some of their collaborating partners include Millennium Pharmaceuticals, Immunex, Pharmacia & Upjohn and Roche.

Largest Biotechnology Discovery Platform

Amgen Inc. (Headquarters)
Amgen Center

Thousand Oaks, CA 91320-1799
(805) 447-1000
CEO Kevin Sharer
Web Site www.amgen.com

Amgen's goal is to be the world leader in developing and delivering important, cost-effective therapeutics based on advances in cellular and molecular biology. Their primary focus includes: genomics, cancer biology and neuroscience, and small molecule chemistry. Amgen is currently marketing four products: Epogen, used to treat anemia associated with chronic renal failure for dialysis patients; Infergen, used to treat hepatitis C; Neupogen, which stimulates the production of white blood cells that help cancer patients taking Myelosuppressive Chemotherapy; and Stemgen, blood-cell growth factor used in patients with aplastic anemia. They currently have at least eleven products in Phase I–III testing with treatments in the areas of oncology, neurobiology, endocrinology, bone and inflammation.

PCs, Servers and More Over the Internet

Dell Computer Corp.
Dell Investor Relations
One Dell Way
Round Rock, TX 78682
(512) 728-7800
CEO Michael Dell
Web Site www.Dell.com

Dell is the worldwide leader in workstation market share and has been rapidly gaining market share here and in the server market. Dell has lowered revenue growth forecasts to 20% for its next fiscal year, but it has continued to gain market share on its rivals in a modestly slowing market. Dell has already revolutionized the computer industry by selling directly to the customer and building its computers to order. Dell is actually one of the leaders in Internet retailing. The "build-to-order and ship-direct" strategy has helped the company avoid being caught with excess inventory when older computers have fallen out of favor. A relentless focus on the customer has also helped Dell stay on top of shifting trends in the computer industry.

Dell recently announced that it would partner with Microsoft to develop advanced server appliances specially designed for network-attached storage (NAS). This market appears to hold great potential for the company as the NAS market is growing rapidly. Prices are still quite high for NAS servers compared to regular PCs. Dell is also setting up a B2B digital exchange, Dell Marketplace, for its customers, that will link up with Ariba's network.

Buying the Stock

A Personal Note To Our Reader

It's important to note that *these stocks should be part of a balanced portfolio and represent only a portion of an overall balanced portfolio.* Because of the huge growth potential of each stock, these stocks are quite volatile. It's one thing to know which stocks can change the world. It's another to know when to buy them.

You must plan for failure! There is a chance that several of these companies will not make it and you must plan for that—in fact, you might want to expect it. It's like planned obsolescence for your portfolio. Let's say you invest $20,000 in a portfolio divided equally between each of the Ten Stocks that Could Change the World. What would your return be in five years if you have nine stocks break even and only one stock that goes up 90% per year (compounded)? Would you believe 28% annualized? What would your return be in ten years if you have nine stocks break even and only one stock that goes up 90% per year (compounding)? Would you believe 51% annualized? A $20,000 portfolio annualizing 51% over ten years becomes $1,244,000 (without regard to taxes).

My point is that in order for you to have a few super-performing stocks, you must accept the fact that a few of the stocks are going to tank! In order for you to build a focused portfolio of stocks that could significantly outperform the market, there must be the strong possibility of failure (being wrong about a stock) built into your portfolio. Without this strong possibility of failure, your portfolio doesn't have much of a chance of significantly beating the market.

THESE STOCKS ARE VOLATILE.

If they weren't, they would not have the potential for the returns you're wanting. Some of these stocks may seem outrageously priced. In March of 2000, Ariba was selling at 250 times revenue and that is certainly outrageous. However, this phenomenon should tell you something about the popularity and following of this stock and its industry B2B. The stock dropped over 60%, ran back up 200% and fell again over 60%. THIS IS VOLATILITY! There are many considerations that should be taken before a prospective investor commits a significant amount of money to a portfolio of very volatile stocks. Investors should think very carefully before committing retirement funds to a strategy like this. IT WOULD BE INAPPROPRIATE TO COMMIT MUCH MORE THAN 10% OF YOUR RETIREMENT SAVINGS TO A STRATEGY LIKE THIS! Also, you should be prepared to ride a two- to three-year period of poor performance (multi-year bear markets can still happen). Investors must take at least a five-plus-year time horizon when buying extremely volatile stocks.

Remember that to win the game it helps to buy right. Here are a couple of suggestions you might want to consider. First, one of the best times to buy these stocks is when the NASDAQ market falls back. It happens pretty often so just look for an opportunity. Don't worry about getting in on the exact bottom; just buy on pull-backs (pull-backs of 10% or more from the high for the index constitute a correction). Some of the best investment opportunities that you will ever see will be buying leading stocks in rapidly growing industries as they come out of a correction. Before buying more of a stock that is down sharply, however, you should double-check your thinking on the company. Check the news, using financial news service web sites such as thestreet.com and yahoo.com or work with a financial advisor that you trust who is knowledgeable about the stock. If you are a long-term holder, you really believe in the stock, and it's going up, then buy more when it drops and let it run.

If you have at least $20,000 to put into these stocks, the best place to buy them is through a discount broker like E-Trade, Ameritrade, or Charles Schwab. At each of these firms, you can buy on-line and get a peek at your portfolio twenty-four hours a day via the web. Beware of the commission rates. At Schwab, for example, let's say you have a minimum commission rate of $29 and you purchase $1,000 worth of a stock. Your commission is 2.9% of your purchase price. This is high, but not unbearable. Just keep in mind the amount of commission you are paying.

If you are working with less than $10,000, you may want to take a look at Sharebuilder.com and Folio.com, where you can buy these stocks at very competitive commission rates with very little money. These services are fantastic for the small portfolio manager. However, you are getting the closing price for the day on these stocks instead of the market price the minute you call or buy on-line.

A note about trading: Our philosophy is to buy and hold, not trade much and certainly not day trade. Day trading is a sucker's game, won only by a handful of fortunate people. The large majority of day traders not only under-perform the market, but also lose everything in their portfolio. The wealthiest people I know who made their fortunes in the stock market were individuals who followed a buy-and-hold strategy. I've never met a long-term successful day trader who built his wealth on day trading. Buy and hold is easier, costs less, and makes more sense.

A Final Note

We hope you've enjoyed reading this book. It's our hope that we helped you better understand the future and the possibilities in the stock market—specifically with these stocks. As we've mentioned before, we do not have a crystal ball, and we do not claim to know everything about the market. We do our very best to pick great stocks that we think have the potential to change the world. We are students of the market, and the more we learn, the more we realize how much more there is to know.

Wealthy Wishes!

Appendix

Company Revenue History

Digimarc Revenue History

Calendar Quarters	4Q98	1Q99	2Q99	3Q99	4Q99	1Q00	2Q00	3Q00
Revenue (in $millions)	0.29	1.1	0.99	2.1	2.7	2.6	2.7	3.1
Sequential Growth Rate		279.3%	-10.0%	112.1%	28.6%	-3.7%	3.8%	14.8%
Gross Margin		54.7%	56.7%	55.8%	37.0%	41.2%	32.7%	44.3%

Global Crossing Revenue History

Calendar Quarters	4Q98	1Q99	2Q99	3Q99	4Q99	1Q00	2Q00	3Q00
Revenue (in $millions)	205.2	176.3	188.5	234.6	1,065.5	932.7	918.4	1,013.1
Sequential Growth Rate		-14.1%	6.9%	24.5%	354.2%	-12.5%	-1.5%	10.3%
Gross Margin		60.6%	57.0%	45.0%	46.4%	37.8%	31.3%	40.8%

Avanex Revenue History

Calendar Quarters	2Q99	3Q99	4Q99	1Q00	2Q00	3Q00
Revenue (in $millions)	0.51	4.4	6.5	10.5	19.3	34.8
Sequential Growth Rate		762.7%	47.7%	61.5%	83.8%	80.3%
Gross Margin		22.7%	26.2%	35.2%	41.5%	44.5%

Inktomi Revenue History

Calendar Quarters	4Q98	1Q99	2Q99	3Q99	4Q99	1Q00	2Q00	3Q00
Revenue (in $millions)	15.2	14.6	19.6	26.2	36.1	47.3	61.5	78.6
Sequential Growth Rate		-3.9%	34.2%	33.7%	37.8%	31.0%	30.0%	27.8%
Gross Margin		85.5%	86.4%	83.2%	83.7%	85.4%	86.3%	86.3%

InfoSpace Revenue History

Calendar Quarters	4Q98	1Q99	2Q99	3Q99	4Q99	1Q00	2Q00	3Q00
Revenue (in $millions)	4.0	5.1	6.7	10.1	14.4	19.0	24.6	57.7
Sequential Growth Rate		27.5%	31.4%	50.7%	42.6%	31.9%	29.5%	134.6%
Gross Margin	84.3%	83.0%	83.3%	85.5%	87.8%	83.6%	81.8%	82.0%

Ariba Revenue History

Calendar Quarters	4Q98	1Q99	2Q99	3Q99	4Q99	1Q00	2Q00	3Q00
Revenue (in $millions)	6.9	9.5	11.9	17.1	23.5	40.0	80.7	134.9
Sequential Growth Rate		37.7%	25.3%	43.7%	37.4%	70.2%	101.8%	67.2%
Gross Margin		81.0%	79.5%	78.9%	85.3%	83.9%	82.7%	82.5%

Docent Revenue History

Calendar Quarters	2Q99*	3Q99*	4Q99*	1Q00*	2Q00*	3Q00*
Revenue (in $millions)	0.086	0.2	0.4	1.0	1.5	2.9
Sequential Growth Rate		132.6%	100.0%	150.0%	50.0%	93.3%
Gross Margin	neg.*	neg.	0.0%	neg.*	neg.*	38.1%

* WCI estimated from 6 month figures

WebEx Revenue History

Calendar Quarters	4Q98	1Q99	2Q99	3Q99	4Q99	1Q00	2Q00	3Q00
Revenue (in $millions)		0.5	0.6	0.4	1.1	2.2	4.5	7.5
Sequential Growth Rate			17.5%	-19.1%	155.6%	93.9%	103.6%	6.7%
Gross Margin			81.7%	68.8%	66.4%	70.2%	64.2%	57.0%

Celera Revenue History

Calendar Quarters	2Q99	3Q99	4Q99	1Q00	2Q00	3Q00
Revenue (in $millions)	5.1	8.3	8.3	11.1	15.0	18.3
Sequential Growth Rate		62.7%	0.0%	3.7%	35.1%	22.0%

Millennium Revenue History

Calendar Quarters	4Q98	1Q99	2Q99	3Q99	4Q99	1Q00	2Q00	3Q00
Revenue (in $millions)	58.0	41.0	47.3	40.3	55.1	46.8	46.9	49.8
Sequential Growth Rate		-29.3%	15.4%	-14.8%	36.7%	-15.1%	0.2%	6.2%